GREENFEAST

SPRING, SUMMER

Also by Nigel Slater:

The Christmas Chronicles
The Kitchen Diaries III: A Year of Good Eating
Eat
The Kitchen Diaries II
Tender, Volumes I and II
Eating for England
The Kitchen Diaries I
Toast – the story of a boy's hunger
Appetite
Real Food
Real Cooking
The 30-Minute Cook
Real Fast Food

Nigel Slater is an award-winning author, journalist and television presenter. He has been food columnist for the *Observer* for over twenty-five years. His collection of bestselling books includes the classics *Appetite* and *The Kitchen Diaries* and the critically acclaimed two-volume *Tender*. He has made cookery programmes and documentaries for BBC1, BBC2 and BBC4. His memoir *Toast – the story of a boy's hunger* won six major awards and is now a film and stage production. His writing has won the James Beard Award, the National Book Award, the Glenfiddich Trophy, the André Simon Memorial Prize and the British Biography of the Year. He lives in London.

nigelslater.com
Twitter @nigelslater
Instagram @nigelslater

GREENFEAST

SPRING, SUMMER

Nigel Slater

Photography by
Jonathan Lovekin

4th ESTATE • *London*

4th Estate
An imprint of HarperCollins*Publishers*
1 London Bridge Street
London SE1 9GF
www.4thEstate.co.uk

First published in Great Britain by 4th Estate in 2019

1 3 5 7 9 8 6 4 2

ISBN 978-0-00-833335-5

Design by David Pearson

Typeset by GS Typesetting

Printed in Neografia, Slovakia

MIX
Paper from
responsible sources
FSC C007454

This book is produced from independently certified FSC paper to ensure
responsible forest management.

Find out more about HarperCollins and the environment at
www.harpercollins.co.uk/green

For James

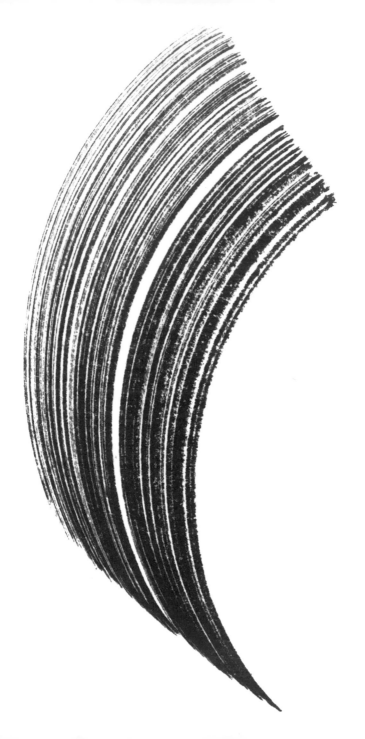

Tom Kemp

Tom Kemp trained as a calligrapher, absorbing the large number of Western scripts written with a quill pen. It was an introduction to the square-edged brush, however, which led to his current work. He studied the heavily-doubted theory that the best classical Roman inscriptions were first written with the brush directly and swiftly on marble; the subsequent carving was just a way of fixing this handwriting in place. Tom rediscovered many of the techniques needed to prove the theory, summarising his findings in a book, *Formal Brush Writing*, published in 1999. Since then he has taught this Roman calligraphic technique in classes around the world. At the same time, he started to explore the idea of writing itself and began to abstract away from letters and words, resulting in what he calls 'writing without language'. Seven years ago, he began to learn the craft of pottery which he now uses to make complex, curved porcelain surfaces on which he writes.

tomkemp.com
Instagram @tom_kemp_

Contents

INTRODUCTION

There is a little black book on the kitchen table. Neatly annotated in places, virtually illegible in others, it is the latest in a long line of tissue-thin pages containing the hand-written details of everything I eat. This is not one of the kitchen chronicles where I write down recipe workings and shopping lists, ideas and wish lists, but a daily diary of everything that ends up on my plate. If I have yoghurt, blackcurrant compote and pumpkin seeds at breakfast it will be in that little book. Likewise, a lunch of green lentils and grilled red peppers or a dinner of roast cauliflower and a bowl of miso soup. Each bowl of soup, plate of pasta and every mushroom on toast is faithfully logged. I don't know exactly why or when I started noting down my dinner, but these little books are now filled in out of habit as much as anything else. The notes are often made at night, just before I lock up and go to bed. I suspect my little black books will be buried with me.

I occasionally look back at what I have written, often as I change one journal for the next. One of the points that interests me, and perhaps this is the main reason I have kept the daily ritual going for so long, is that I can follow how my eating has changed, albeit gradually, over the years. There are of course unshakable edibles, (I seem to have started and ended each day's eating with a bowl of yoghurt for as long as I can remember), but I also find marked changes in what I cook and eat. The most notable is the quantity, I definitely eat less than I used to, and there is a conspicuous move towards lighter dishes, particularly in spring and summer.

But here's another thing. Despite being resolutely omnivorous, it is clear how much of my everyday eating has become plant-based. Although not strictly vegetarian (the bottom line for me will always be that my dinner is delicious, not something that must adhere to a set of strict dietary rules), much of my weekday eating contains neither meat nor fish. I am not sure this was a particularly considered choice. It is simply the way my eating has grown to be over the last few years. I do know, however, that I am not alone in this.

Greenfeast, like *Eat* before it, is a collection of what I eat when I finish work every day: the casual yet spirited meals with which I sustain myself and whoever else is around. The recipes are, like those in previous collections, more for inspiration than rules to be adhered to, slavishly, word for word. But unlike *Eat*, this collection offers no meat or fish. The idea of collecting these recipes together is for those like-minded eaters who find themselves wanting inspiration for a supper that owes more to plants than animals.

HOW I EAT

I rarely hand someone a plate full of food. More hospitable and more fun, I think, is a table that has a selection of bowls and dishes of food to which people can help themselves. And by that, I mean dinner for two or three as much as those for a group of family or friends. That way, the table comes to life, food is offered or passed round, a dish is shared, the meal is instantly more joyful.

In summer there will be a couple of light, easily-prepared principal dishes. Alongside those will be some sort of accompaniment. There may be wedges of toasted sourdough, glossy with olive oil and flakes of sea salt. Noodles that I have cooked, often by simply pouring boiling water over them, then tossed in a little toasted sesame oil and coriander leaves, or an all-singing and -dancing Korean chilli paste.

A dish of red pepper soup might sit alongside a plate of fried aubergines and feta. Crisp pea croquettes may well be placed on the table with tomato and French bean salad. Southeast-Asian noodles might be eaten with roast spring vegetables and peanut sauce and a mild dish of creamed and grilled cauliflower could turn up with a spiced tomato couscous. Two dishes, often three, are very much the usual at home. I find the thought of being able to dip into several dishes uplifting in comparison to a single plate piled high.

Much of what I cook in the spring and summer is exceptionally light, by which I mean it is unlikely to be carb-heavy or based on dairy produce. There are a few things that come out on a regular basis. Bowls of yoghurt that have been folded through with chopped mint and coriander, a splash of rice vinegar and chives. There are often some lightly pickled vegetables: usually carrots, beetroot or red onions. A tangle of sauerkraut turned with an equal volume of chopped herbs, or a tomato and basil salad. Like migratory birds, these are regular visitors to my summer table. There will be others too. Perhaps some rice with crisped onions and coriander or noodles tossed with crushed tomatoes, sea salt and red wine vinegar. There may be a dish of couscous with mint, golden sultanas and green peas, or new potatoes with olive oil, tarragon and lemon zest.

It is no secret that I have a deep affection for the cold months, but my love of summer cooking, its ease and laidback feeling is not far behind. There are highlights that turn up on the table from May to September and often beyond. A few pieces of melon rolled in the juice of a passion fruit for breakfast. A deep cup of miso soup with shreds of spring greens and lemon for lunch. The uppermost points of early summer asparagus tossed with ground sesame seeds and a trickle of toasted oil to accompany a salad of sprouted seeds and green peas. A single misshapen ball of burrata with an emerald ribbon of basil oil, or a cucumber, crushed and scattered with cool ricotta and mint leaves aside a bowl of avocado and green wheat. The list is almost endless.

The recipes throughout the book are light. They are meant to be mixed and matched as you wish. A table with several little bowls of light, unfussy food to please and delight and, ultimately, gently sustain.

A NOTE ON THE RECIPES

Though all are plant-based, the recipes within these pages are not strictly vegetarian. They can, however, be rendered suitable for vegetarian or vegan diets with a bit of informed tweaking.

IN A BOWL

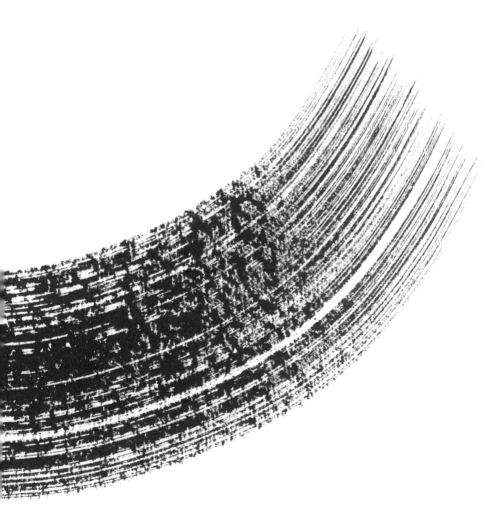

I am a collector of bowls. Bowls for soup and porridge, bowls for rice and pasta, bowls for pudding. I enjoy choosing which will be most appropriate for my dinner, deep or shallow, with a rim or without, earthenware, lacquer or wood. There is nothing precious about this, I simply feel that food tastes better when you eat it from something that flatters the contents.

When I moved to London, forty years ago, I bought a couple of thick, heavy, white Pillivuyt soup bowls. I have them to this day. They were my only tableware for many years, long before I bought plates or shallow dishes. They are used daily, no longer to eat from, but for beating eggs or blending a dressing. There is always at least one sitting in the fridge, a saucer for a hat, keeping a little treasure safe for another day.

I have two wooden bowls for porridge, made from ash. They form a gentle start to the day. The quiet, beatific pleasure of the movement of wooden spoon across wooden bowl. I feel like Goldilocks, even when they are used for a strawberry Bircher muesli. Occasionally they are commandeered for a soup or rice, but they are without doubt meant for the early hours.

Miso broth is my panacea. It solves every question, soothes every ill, warms, satiates and cossets. Initially a morning ritual, the bowl of miso soup can be enhanced with sliced vegetables, shreds of seaweed, sliced mushrooms and skeins of noodles. If ever I am unsure of what I want to eat, five minutes with a cup of miso broth and I have decided. The darker the miso the more it sharpens the appetite and spurs you to cook.

Serving risotto from a bowl instead of a plate is enough to get you lynched in some circles. I care not a jot. I like my risotto in a bowl, where the last spoonful (and yes, a spoon!) remains as hot as the first rather than chilling on a plate. Or perhaps it is the joy that springs from winding up those whose eating is atrophied by tradition. That said, I am not a prolific eater of rice. There is much to be said though for a bowl of pure white basmati or sticky Japanese rice, seasoned with jewel-coloured tsukemono, the emerald, saffron and magenta pickles of Kyoto. Sometimes, I crumble a sheet of nori over the top, or sprinkle the tiny tea-green flakes over the grains, or add a dusting of chilli and sesame-toasted togarishi.

The holding of a bowl – more like cradling really – comforts us. But it is important how the bowl feels in the hand. Too rough and it can grate on the nerves, like nails down a blackboard or teeth on a pear drop. Too smooth and your soup feels refined and cold-hearted. What I appreciate most is the humble quality of a bowl and the food you put in it. Even the most exquisitely-formed recipe is brought down a peg or two when served in an earthenware dish. The food jumbles unaffectedly in the hollow, the deep sides capture the scent of the food, increasing the enjoyment of every mouthful.

I eat more food from a bowl than I do from a plate. Partly because I can pick it up and get closer to my food, the act of eating becomes more intimate, but also because of my adoration of potters and the work that goes into their art and craft. The idea that something has been on a clay-dusted wheel, moulded and shaped by their own hands and signed with a potter's mark, only adds to the experience. The only ones that don't work for me are the square ones, angular, awkward and uncomfortable and no less unattractive than square plates. A bright pattern can cheer or jar as your spirit takes you.

This being a spring and summer book, there are probably fewer bowl-based recipes than in the second autumn and winter volume, but we still have a crisp Vietnamese-inspired salad, a cooling melon gazpacho, a paneer korma and a bowl of green peas and sprouted seeds. There are rice bowls and soup bowls, freekeh salad, a verdant curry and a deep dish of creamy noodles. There are others of course, recipes in the On the Hob chapter in particular. There is not much that isn't more appealing to me when eaten from the depths of a beautiful bowl.

I don't think we should spend too much time agonising over the right receptacle for the right food any more than we should play too seriously the wine-matching game. That said, I get pleasure from rummaging through my collection of everyday, utilitarian pieces simply to make my food look comfortable. (Anyone who has ever put tomato soup into a bright blue dish will know what uncomfortable food looks like.) In general, salads need a bit more space so I tend to favour a wide dish. Big soups like a generous home in which to sit – it will keep the contents hotter for longer and shallow ones are good for beautiful ingredients you want to admire. A deep one will also give you the joy of finding a hidden dumpling lurking deliciously at the bottom.

I have a certain reverence for food served in a bowl that I don't when it is served on a plate. I am not sure why this should be, I only know that it is. I love the way the dressing, sauce or juices sit in the base, to be spooned up as a final treat, which is why so many of the dishes throughout these books are presented the way they are. It is my preferred way to eat.

CHICKPEA, PEA, SPROUTED SEEDS

A can of chickpeas from the shelf. Green peas from the freezer. A store-cupboard supper for a spring evening.

Serves 4

chickpeas 2 × 400g cans

frozen or fresh peas 400g
  (podded weight)

sprouted mung beans 100g

sprouted seeds such as radish 80g

olive oil 4 tablespoons

ground cumin 2 teaspoons

ground coriander 2 teaspoons

For the dressing:

tahini 1 tablespoon

juice of a lemon

olive oil 4 tablespoons

Bring a pan of water to the boil. Drain and rinse the chickpeas. Cook the peas in boiling water till tender. Drain and refresh in a bowl of iced water. Rinse the mung beans and sprouted seeds in cold water and shake them dry.

Make the dressing: beat together the tahini, lemon juice and olive oil.

Warm the olive oil in a frying pan over a moderate heat, add the chickpeas and ground spices and let them sizzle for a couple of minutes till hot and fragrant. Move the chickpeas around the pan as they brown.

Drain the peas again and put them in a serving bowl with the mung beans and radish sprouts. Fold in the dressing and lastly the chickpeas.

• One of those everlastingly useful 'suppers in minutes'. Use frozen peas or a packet of fresh, podded peas from the supermarket. If you are podding fresh peas for this you will need a generous kilo.

• Use whichever sprouted peas you have around, including the mixtures of lentils and mung beans from health food shops. The point is to introduce as many differing textures as you can.

FREEKEH, PEACHES, FETA

Sweet-salty cheese and fruit. The comfort of warm grain.

Serves 2–3

freekeh 125g

thyme a few sprigs

bay leaves 2

feta 250g

za'atar 1 teaspoon

a large peach

olive oil 3 tablespoons

a medium onion

mint 10g

parsley 20g

a lemon

Set the oven at 200°C/Gas 6. Put the freekeh, thyme and bay on to boil with enough water to cover by a good third. Salt it lightly and simmer for fifteen minutes.

Place a large piece of kitchen foil on a baking sheet, lay the piece of feta in the middle and sprinkle with the za'atar. Halve the peach, discard the stone, then cut each half into four. Tuck the peach around the feta, then pour over two tablespoons of the olive oil. Pull the sides of the foil up around its cargo and scrunch loosely to seal. Bake for twenty minutes.

Peel and finely slice the onion, then fry till crisp in the reserved oil. Set aside on kitchen paper.

Chop the mint and parsley together. Remove the feta from the oven and open the parcel. Pour the baking juices out into a bowl and mix with the juice of the lemon. Drain the freekeh, discarding the herbs, then dress with the lemon and baking juices. Fold in the mint and parsley, then break up the feta into large pieces and add. Lay the peaches amongst the freekeh, top with the crisp onions and serve.

• A substantial salad of warm, chewy grain, salty cheese and sweet, juicy peaches. The parsley and mint are important, but you could use basil too, or even coriander if you prefer.

GREENS, COCONUT CURRY

Vibrant, verdant.

Serves 2–4

For the curry paste:
white peppercorns 1 teaspoon
coriander seeds 1 teaspoon
ground turmeric 1 teaspoon
lemon grass 2 stalks
garlic 2 cloves
ginger a 3cm lump, peeled
hot green chillies 3 small
groundnut oil 3 tablespoons
fresh coriander a handful,
   with roots

groundnut oil 1 tablespoon
vegetable stock 200ml
coconut milk 250ml
fish sauce 1 tablespoon
lime juice 2 tablespoons
spring vegetables (such as
   asparagus tips, broad beans,
   peas) 450g total weight
shredded greens, such as spring
   cabbage a handful
pinch of sugar and soy sauce

For the paste, put the white peppercorns and coriander seeds in a dry non-stick frying pan and toast lightly for two or three minutes, then tip into the bowl of a food processor and add half a teaspoon of sea salt, the turmeric, lemon grass, peeled garlic cloves, ginger, green chillies, three tablespoons of groundnut oil and a handful of coriander stems and roots. Blitz to a coarse paste. You can keep this paste for a few days in the fridge, its surface covered with groundnut oil to prevent it drying out.

In a deep pan, fry three lightly heaped tablespoons of the curry paste in a tablespoon of oil for thirty seconds till fragrant, stirring as you go. Stir in the vegetable stock and coconut milk, the fish sauce and lime juice.

Add the asparagus tips, broad beans and peas and continue simmering for five to six minutes, then drop in a couple of handfuls of greens, shredded into thick ribbons. Finish the curry with a pinch of sugar, fish sauce, a little soy sauce and more lime.

MELON, PEPPERS, CUCUMBER

Cold fruit soup. Refreshing. A deep scent of summer.

Serves 6

Romano peppers 3
a large yellow pepper
cucumber 250g
cantaloupe melon, ripe 1.25kg
   (unpeeled weight)

basil 10g
sherry vinegar 1 tablespoon
half a lemon
ice cubes

Halve and seed the peppers, then cut them into large pieces. Coarsely mince or process them to your preferred consistency, then put them in a large bowl. I prefer quite a smooth soup, but others like a more robust texture. Peel the cucumber and cut into rough chunks, then process to the same texture as the peppers and add to the bowl. Prepare the melon, discarding the skin, seeds and fibre, then cutting the flesh into chunks. Process in a similar way to the other ingredients, then mix with the peppers and cucumber.

Roughly chop the basil and stir into the soup together with the sherry vinegar, lemon juice and a little salt and black pepper. Cover and chill thoroughly. Stir in the ice cubes just before serving.

• A light, bright-tasting soup to serve chilled. By which I mean thoroughly cold and with ice cubes. The consistency can be as smooth or rough as you like, but I prefer it to have a coarse texture, so I use the mincer attachment to the food mixer. I have used a food processor too, but a careful eye is required to avoid reducing it to a purée.

MISO, CAULIFLOWER, GINGER

Gentle soup for a spring day. The warmth of toasted garlic and ginger.

Serves 2

cauliflower 150g

garlic 2 cloves

ginger 30g

groundnut oil 2 tablespoons

dark miso paste 2 tablespoons

light miso paste 2 tablespoons

mirin 2 tablespoons

Cut the cauliflower into florets, then slice them thinly. Peel and thinly slice the garlic. Peel the ginger and cut into matchsticks.

Warm the groundnut oil in a shallow pan, then fry the garlic and ginger for a couple of minutes until pale and soft. Add the cauliflower, turning it over from time to time, letting it cook for four or five minutes until the slices colour lightly. By the time the cauliflower is cooked, the garlic should be a deep honey gold. Divide the cauliflower, garlic and ginger between four bowls.

Bring 1 litre of water to the boil, then stir in the miso pastes and the mirin. Simmer for two minutes, then ladle into the bowls over the cauliflower.

MISO, MUSHROOMS, PAK CHOI

Light, savoury, sustaining. A little bowl of calm.

Serves 4

sugar snap peas or shelled peas 150g
vegetable or chicken stock 750ml
white miso paste 4 tablespoons
spring onions 3
pak choi 125g

enoki mushrooms 100g
Thai basil a small bunch
a lime
light soy sauce

Bring a medium-sized pan of water to the boil. Add the sugar snaps or shelled peas and let them boil for two minutes, then lift them out with a slotted spoon and drop them into a bowl of cold water.

Warm the stock in a large pan. When the stock is hot, add the miso, stirring until it has dissolved. The stock should be very hot but not boiling. Finely slice the spring onions and add half to the stock. Halve the pak choi and push the pieces down into the stock. Remove and discard the roots from the enoki mushrooms, then add to the stock too.

Tear up the Thai basil leaves. Squeeze the juice from the lime. Divide the hot broth between four bowls, and add the remaining spring onions, the peas, basil leaves and the lime juice. Pass soy sauce around at the table, leaving everyone to season as they wish.

• Clear, light, gentle. I look upon this as something for those moments when you want a bowl of soup that is quietly sustaining rather than filling. A full-flavoured vegetable stock is essential, as is a generous hand with the seasoning. I tend to use chicken stock for this. I would leave the addition of soy sauce to individual diners. Just a little for me please, as I find soy sauce all too easily dominates everything in its path.

BULGUR, NECTARINES, PARSLEY

The comfort of grains. The sweetness of ripe fruit. The vibrancy of lemon and parsley.

Serves 2–3, as a main dish

vegetable or chicken stock or
    water 75ml
bulgur wheat 50g
radishes, mixed colours 20

nectarines, ripe 2
parsley 100g
juice of a large lemon
watercress 50g

Bring the stock or water to the boil. Put the bulgur in a heatproof bowl, pour over the hot stock or water, then set aside.

Trim and thinly slice the radishes and put them into a mixing bowl. Halve the nectarines, discard the stones, then finely dice the flesh into (roughly) 1cm cubes. Add to the radishes, then remove the parsley leaves from their stalks, chop finely and fold in.

Season the radishes and nectarines lightly with salt, then add the lemon juice. Drain any excess liquid from the bulgur, run a fork through the grains to separate them, then fold into the salad. Pile the watercress onto a serving dish, then spoon the bulgur on top and serve.

• Tabbouleh, of which this is a version, comes in many guises, but the most interesting are those that have far more parsley than grain. The herbs and fruit lend an essential lushness.

PANEER, AUBERGINE, CASHEWS

Gentle spice for a summer's evening.

Serves 2–3 with rice or flatbread
For the spice mix:

garlic 2 cloves, peeled
ginger 20g, after peeling
ground turmeric 2 teaspoons
garam masala 2 teaspoons
ground coriander 2 teaspoons
ground cumin 2 teaspoons
cardamom pods 6
ground chilli 1 teaspoon

groundnut or olive oil
    4 tablespoons
double cream 250ml
aubergine, medium 1
vegetable oil 3 tablespoons
paneer 200g
cashew nuts 100g
natural yoghurt 150ml
coriander leaves a small handful

Make the spice mix by grinding the garlic, ginger, turmeric, garam masala, ground coriander, cumin and the black seeds from inside the cardamom pods to a paste in a food processor or blender. Add the chilli and groundnut oil. Cook the paste over a low heat for four or five minutes, then stir in the double cream and a little salt. Set aside.

Cut the aubergine into 3cm cubes, then fry in the vegetable oil till soft and golden. Tear the paneer into rough pieces and add to the aubergine with the cashews, letting the nuts and paneer colour lightly. Add the warm spiced cream to the mixture, get it hot, then remove from the heat and stir in the yoghurt and the coriander leaves. Serve with warm flatbread.

• I sometimes add a pinch of sugar to the spice paste, softening the spices and producing a more mellow flavour.
• Rather than aubergine, I often use brown chestnut mushrooms instead, slicing them thickly and frying them in the oil before adding the paneer.

PAPAYA, CARROT, RADISH

The crunch of carrots. The warmth of radish and the honey-sweetness of ripe papaya.

Serves 4

radishes 12
carrots, medium 3
papaya, ripe 350g
coriander leaves from
    12 bushy stems
micro herbs 2 handfuls
Thai basil leaves 15

For the dressing:
palm sugar 3 teaspoons
rice vinegar 2 tablespoons
a juicy lime
lemon grass 2 stalks
fish sauce 3 teaspoons

Make the dressing: crumble the palm sugar into a small mixing bowl and pour in the rice vinegar. Halve the lime – I like to roll it on the work surface, pressing down firmly as I do so before slicing, you get more juice that way – then squeeze the juice into the sugar and vinegar. Season with salt and stir until the sugar has dissolved.

Place the lemon grass on a chopping board and bash firmly with a rolling pin to split and crush the plump end of the stalks. Add them to the dressing with the fish sauce and leave for thirty minutes to infuse.

Halve the radishes and put them into a bowl of iced water. Scrub or peel the carrots, then shave them with a vegetable peeler into long thin shavings. Add them to the radishes.

Shortly before serving, when the radishes and carrots have spent twenty minutes in the iced water and the dressing is well infused, peel the papaya and discard the black seeds and fibres. Slice the fruit into small, thick pieces about the size of a stamp and put them in a large mixing bowl.

Pick the leaves from the coriander and add them to the papaya together with the micro herbs (leaves and stalks) and the whole Thai basil leaves.

(continued)

Dry the carrots in a salad spinner, then toss them and the radishes with the papaya and herbs. Discard the lemon grass stalks and pour the dressing over the papaya before tossing the ingredients gently together, taking care not to crush the fruit.

• I find the large papayas, usually sold in halves, best for salads. They seem to ripen better than the smaller fruit. Their flesh is more luscious. The downside is apparent when you realise that your purchase takes up an entire shelf in the fridge.

In a bowl 25

PEAS, PARSLEY, VEGETABLE STOCK

A green soup for a sunny day.

Serves 4, generously

butter 30g	peas 200g (shelled weight)
spring onions 75g	garlic 2 cloves
flat-leaf parsley 300g	vegetable or chicken stock
a medium potato	1 litre

Melt the butter in a large, heavy-based pan. Chop the spring onions and stir them into the butter, letting them cook for four to five minutes over a moderate heat.

Chop half the parsley, stalks and all, add it to the spring onions and leave to cook for a minute or two till the colour has darkened. Peel, dice and add the potato. Add the peas and peeled garlic and pour in the stock. Bring to the boil, then lower the heat to a simmer and cook for eight to ten minutes.

Put a pan of water on to boil. Discard the stalks from the reserved parsley, add the leaves to the boiling water and leave for two minutes, then drain. Stir the leaves into the soup, then remove from the heat and reduce to a smooth, green purée in a blender or food processor and serve.

• The brilliant vibrancy of this soup appeals here, but you could soften its healthy green edges by stirring in 100ml of double cream at the end. Take care not to overfill the blender in case the hot soup overflows. I only say this because I invariably do.

PEPPERS, CHICKPEAS, GARLIC

Earthy and garlicky. A smooth cream for warm flatbread.

Serves 4, as a side dish

red peppers 500g
olive oil
garlic 6 cloves
chickpeas 2 × 400g cans

thyme 4 sprigs
bay leaves 2
paprika a pinch or two

Set the oven at 200°C/Gas 6. Slice the peppers in half lengthways, remove the seeds, then place the halves in a roasting tin. Trickle a little olive oil over the peppers, just enough to wet them, then set the unpeeled garlic cloves inside them. Bake for forty minutes or until they are soft and the skin somewhat blackened. Remove from the oven, then peel away their outer skins. Reserve the garlic and any juices in the roasting tin.

Drain and rinse the chickpeas, pop them from their skins if you wish, then tip them into a saucepan, add the thyme and bay and cover with water. Bring to the boil, lower the heat, then simmer for fifteen minutes.

Drain the cooked chickpeas, reserve the thyme (discard the bay), then tip all but a handful of the chickpeas into the bowl of a food processor with the roasted, skinned peppers. Add the thyme leaves (discard the stalks) then pop the roasted garlic from its skin and add it as well. Process to a smooth cream and season generously with salt and black pepper. Scoop the paste out into a serving dish, making a hollow in the centre with the back of a spoon.

Heat the reserved chickpeas in a little olive oil in a frying pan and cook for a few minutes till they start to turn gold. Pour a little olive oil over the paste, letting it trickle into the hollow, scatter the warm chickpeas over the surface, then dust lightly with the paprika. *(continued)*

• A hummus of sorts. (I am uncomfortable with calling something by that name that contains anything other than chickpeas, garlic, lemon and oil.) I do think it is worth skinning the chickpeas (I know, I know, but once you have done so, you may never look back). You can do it painstakingly, pea by pea, or simply rub them together in your palms, a handful at a time. Either way will result in a smoother mash. Your call.

• I have been known to sit with this and a pile of warm Turkish pitta, but it is also a fine side dish for cold roast meats, grilled aubergines, and my favourite, deep-fried artichokes.

POMEGRANATE, CUCUMBER, PUFFED RICE

Aromatic, crunchy, refreshing.

Serves 4, as a side salad

a small pomegranate
cucumber 400g
coriander seeds 1 teaspoon
cumin seeds 1 teaspoon
groundnut oil 2 tablespoons
garam masala 1 teaspoon
curry powder 1 teaspoon

almonds 50g, whole and skinned
chickpeas 1 × 400g can
hemp seeds 30g
sunflower seeds 30g
puffed rice, unsweetened 30g
parsley a handful
olive oil

Crack open the pomegranate and remove the seeds, putting them into a mixing bowl and discarding any white pith as you go. Peel the cucumber, lightly, leaving as much colour as you can, then cut in half lengthways. Scrape out the seeds and pith with a teaspoon and discard, then cut the flesh into small dice. Toss the cucumber and pomegranate together.

Put the coriander and cumin seeds in a shallow pan and warm them over a gentle heat. Let them cook, moving them around the pan, until crisp and fragrant. Remove the pan from the heat and tip the toasted seeds into a mortar. Crush them to a fine powder.

Warm the groundnut oil in the shallow pan, then, keeping the heat low, add the coriander and cumin, garam masala and curry powder, then the almonds. Warm the nuts and spices, moving everything round the pan so it doesn't burn. Drain and rinse the chickpeas and stir them into the spices and almonds, together with the hemp and sunflower seeds and the puffed rice. Tear the parsley leaves from their stalks and add to the bowl. Tip the warm chickpea mixture into the pomegranate and cucumber, add a trickle of olive oil, then toss gently together and serve.

QUINOA, PEAS, SPROUTED SEEDS

Soft leaves, crunchy, lightly cooked peas. The knubby quality of quinoa.

Serves 6

quinoa 100g
peas 400g (weight with pods)
sprouted mung, sunflower and
   radish seeds 100g
cress a small punnet
micro leaves and marigold petals
   a large handful

For the dressing:

pomegranate molasses
   2 tablespoons
lemon juice 2 tablespoons
olive oil 2 tablespoons

Put the quinoa into a pan with 175ml of water and bring to the boil. Reduce the heat and simmer for six minutes before turning off the heat and leaving, covered, for twenty minutes.

Pod the peas and cook them in deep, lightly salted boiling water for four minutes or until they are almost tender. (They are good when slightly undercooked.) Drain and plunge them into iced water.

Mix the pomegranate molasses, lemon juice and olive oil together in a large mixing bowl and season lightly. Run a fork through the quinoa to separate the grains, then tip into the dressing.

Wash the sprouted seeds in a sieve in cold running water and shake dry. Mix the peas, seeds, cress, micro leaves and petals with the quinoa and its dressing and serve.

• Once made, this is a good base in which to use other leftovers, torn into juicy pieces, or simply to put on the table with other dishes. I should add that it makes a sound addition to lunchboxes, and will be fine in the fridge for a couple of days.

RICE, BROAD BEANS, ASPARAGUS

Homely buttered rice. The luxury of new season's vegetables.

Serves 2–3

broad beans, podded a couple
   of handfuls
asparagus 18 spears

For the pilaf:
white basmati rice 120g
butter 50g
bay leaves 3
green cardamom pods 6
black peppercorns 6

a cinnamon stick
cloves 2 or 3
cumin seeds a pinch
thyme a couple of sprigs

For the herb butter:
mint leaves 8 large
parsley a small handful
spring onions 2
butter, soft 200g

Cook the beans in deep, lightly salted boiling water for three or four minutes. Drain and pop the largest of the beans from their skins. Any very small beans can be left as they are. Trim the asparagus, removing any tough ends, then cut the spears into short lengths. Boil or steam for five or six minutes until just tender.

Wash the rice three times in a bowl of warm water. This will prevent it sticking together. Melt the butter in a saucepan over a moderate heat, add the bay leaves, the cardamom pods, lightly crushed, peppercorns, cinnamon stick, cloves, cumin seeds and sprigs of thyme. Stir the spices and herbs around in the butter for a minute or two, then, as soon as they are warm and fragrant, drain the rice and add it to the pan. Stir the rice to coat it with the butter, then pour in enough water to cover and leave 2cm of water above the rice.

Season with salt, turn down the heat so the water simmers and cover tightly with a lid. After seven minutes, lift the lid, and fold in the drained

(continued)

asparagus and the broad beans. Replace the lid and continue cooking for a further five minutes. Remove from the heat, leave the lid in place and set aside for three minutes.

Make the butter: put the mint leaves on top of one another, roll them up tightly, then shred them finely. Remove the parsley leaves from their stalks and finely chop. Discard the roots and the darkest green shoots of the spring onions. Finely chop the white and pale green part.

Cream the butter until it is soft and fluffy. Season with a little coarsely ground black pepper and sea salt. Fold in the mint, parsley and spring onions.

Lift the lid from the rice, stir with a fork to separate the grains, then fold in the herb butter. Alternatively, divide the rice between plates, place a spoonful of the herb butter on the hot rice and fold in so the grains are coated.

• If you make the butter in advance, remove it from the fridge a good half hour before using. It should be soft and fluffy.

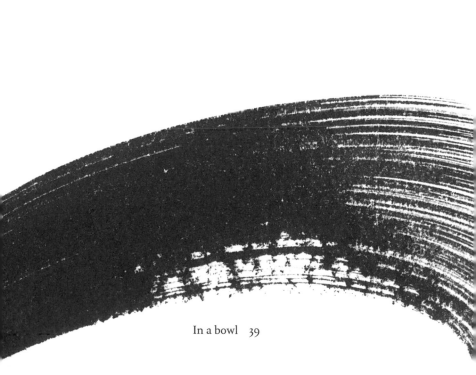

In a bowl   39

RUNNER BEANS, CASHEWS, TOMATOES

Crisp, crunchy, refreshing.

Serves 2

runner beans 350g	cashews 100g
garlic 2 large cloves	cherry tomatoes 300g
guindilla chillies 3	spring onions 3
olive oil 4 tablespoons	

Put a deep pan of water on to boil. Remove any strings from the edges of the runner beans, then cut the beans into short, thick slices. When the water is boiling, salt it lightly and tip in the beans. Let them cook for two minutes, then drain and plunge them into deep, iced water.

Peel and thinly slice the garlic, chop the chillies, then sauté both briefly in the olive oil. Remove and set aside, then return the pan to the heat, add the cashews and let them turn a light golden brown. Remove from the oil and salt generously.

Quarter the tomatoes and chop the spring onions, then toss them with the drained runner beans, garlic, chillies, cashews and a grinding of black pepper.

• A nutty salad for serving alongside other dishes.

SHIITAKE, COCONUT, SOBA NOODLES

Deeply aromatic. Vibrant. Heart-warming.

Serves 2

For the spice paste:
red chillies, small, hot 3
garlic 3 cloves
ginger a 30g lump
lemon grass 3 stalks
coriander seeds 1 teaspoon
coriander leaves a handful
ground turmeric 1 teaspoon
vegetable oil a little

shallots, medium 6
shiitake mushrooms 150g
vegetable stock 500ml
spinach 150g
soba noodles 200g
coconut milk 400ml
coriander leaves, to finish
     a handful

Blend the chillies, garlic, peeled ginger, lemon grass, coriander seeds and leaves, turmeric and a little vegetable oil to a paste in a food processor.

Peel and halve the shallots and halve the shiitake. Warm the spice paste in a wok or frying pan over a moderate heat, then add the shallots and mushrooms. Let everything sizzle for a minute or two, then pour in the stock, bring to the boil, lower the heat and simmer for fifteen minutes.

Wash the spinach and whilst the leaves are wet, cook lightly in a pan with a lid. When they have relaxed, remove to a bowl of iced water to stop them cooking any further. Squeeze almost dry and roughly chop.

Put the noodles into a heatproof bowl, pour over boiling water from the kettle and push the noodles down into the water. Leave for five minutes, then drain. Add the coconut milk to the mushrooms, simmer for five minutes, then add the spinach and noodles. Finish with a little fresh coriander.

RICE, COURGETTES, PICKLED VEGETABLES

Quietly pleasing. Frugal.

Serves 2

sushi rice 180g	pickled ginger 20g
small courgettes 150g	basil leaves a handful
sesame oil 1 tablespoon	coriander leaves a handful
Japanese pickled radish,	dried seaweed flakes 2 tablespoons
pumpkin, etc. 75g	rice vinegar 1 tablespoon

Wash the sushi rice in a bowl of warm water, pour off the water and repeat. Tip the rice into a medium-sized saucepan, pour in 300ml of water and bring to the boil. Lower the heat so the water is simmering, add half a teaspoon of salt, then cover with a lid and leave to cook for fifteen minutes.

Trim the courgettes, then, using a vegetable peeler, remove slices in long, thin shavings. Toss the slices in the sesame oil and season lightly with salt. Roughly chop the Japanese pickled vegetables. Shred the pickled ginger. Roughly chop the basil and coriander leaves.

When the rice is cooked, remove the pan from the heat and leave to rest for five minutes, still covered by its lid. Remove the lid and fold the raw courgettes, chopped pickles and ginger, basil and coriander into the rice with a fork. Stir in the dried seaweed flakes and rice vinegar and season to taste.

• If some rice has stuck to the bottom of the pan during cooking, empty out the rest of the rice, then pour a little water into the pan, bring to the boil and leave it for a minute or two. The rice will be easy to remove.

• The shavings of courgettes soften in the residual heat of the cooked rice. You could stir in a few other good ingredients instead. Chopped tomatoes that you have marinated briefly in olive oil and basil. French beans, lightly cooked and cut into short lengths or, better still, thin batons of cucumber tossed with a little rice wine vinegar and a few nigella seeds.

RICE, PICKLES, NORI

A bowl of steaming rice. The snap of crisp pickles.

Serves 2

carrots 2, large
a banana shallot, medium-sized
mirin 2 tablespoons
rice vinegar 6 tablespoons
tamari soy sauce 1 tablespoon

sushi rice 190g
dried nori flakes 2 teaspoons
tsukemono (pickled vegetables)
  6 teaspoons

Scrub the carrots and slice them into rounds no thicker than a pound coin. Put them into a sealable freezer bag. Peel the shallot, slice thinly, then add to the carrots. Pour the mirin, rice vinegar and soy into the bag and seal it tightly, then refrigerate for at least thirty minutes, though it will keep in good condition for several days.

Wash the rice in warm water, drain, then put it in a small, deep pan, cover with 300ml of cold water and soak for thirty minutes. Bring to the boil, lightly salt, then cover the pot tightly with a lid and simmer for ten minutes. Remove from the heat and leave to rest for another ten minutes, then lift the lid and run a fork through the grains. It will be fluffy and sticky.

Divide the rice between two deep bowls, then sprinkle with the nori flakes and spoon over some of the crisp pickles, the tsukemono and their juice.

IN A PAN

I cook many a meal in a shallow pan over a low flame. I put a low-sided pan on the hob, pour in a little olive oil, warm it until its surface shimmers, then lower in vegetables – asparagus, green beans, mushrooms, fennel or summer squash – followed by a generous splash of water, a trio of bay leaves, half a dozen black peppercorns and a clove or two of young mauve-skinned garlic. The vegetables then cook over a low to moderate heat, partially covered by a lid, till fork tender. I finish them with lemon juice and torn basil or mint and bring them to the table with thick slices of toasted sourdough rubbed with garlic and olive oil. There will, depending on how hungry I am, be a dish of new potatoes steamed, crushed and tossed in soured cream and chives or perhaps some rice, steamed then fried in butter. A light, yet not insubstantial summer dinner.

A frying pan was one of the first pieces of cookware I ever bought. I now have two, a thin, flat, non-stick pan I use for pancakes and the like and a heavy, hardwearing cast-iron version that has a non-stick surface built up from years of active service. The cheaper non-stick pans come and go; the cast-iron pan will, I suspect, pretty much see me out.

A shallow pan is probably the most useful of all, unless you eat a lot of soup or pasta. All manner of good things can shape up for dinner in a frying or sauté pan, from a cake of sweet potato with crushed tomatoes, to bubble and squeak with watercress and dill. Or perhaps a frittata, its thin layer of egg topped with asparagus, finger-thick carrots or shredded spring greens.

Yes, I will fry slices of aubergine in olive oil and serve them with crumbled feta, or fill an omelette with steamed asparagus and tarragon butter, but I am just as likely to fry something in a shallow pan as an accompaniment for a bowl of rice. Tomatoes for instance, cooked down to a scarlet slush over a low flame, crushed under my wooden spoon and seasoned with pepper, basil and parsley until I have a thick jam to spoon over steamed, spiced basmati. I might use such a pan to crisp ready-made gnocchi before tossing them with sharp green-shouldered tomatoes and pink and white radishes, or to fry fennel and young carrots to accompany melted cheese or, for those other than myself, a softly cooked egg.

Having a shallow pan to cook in gives us the gift of speed. Supper in minutes. It is also possibly the most successful way to use leftovers. I have made myself many a fine supper from warming a glug of olive oil and a slice of butter in a pan, then adding 'bits from the fridge' – leftover cooked potato, sautéed vegetables or mushrooms, a few cold noodles or a spoonful of cooked rice, then folding in harissa sauce or several shakes of za'atar. A bit of a mixed bag to be honest, with some compilations more successful than others, but something of a blessing when you come home tired and hungry. Which is of course what this book is for.

ASPARAGUS, BROAD BEANS, EGGS

Light lunch. The first sign of spring.

Serves 2

broad beans 450g
(weight with pods)
asparagus 150g
carrots, slim, young 200g
butter 30g

olive oil
chervil 5g, or parsley leaves 10g
eggs 4
Parmesan, grated 2 tablespoons

Put a pan of water on to boil. Remove the beans from their pods, then cook in boiling, lightly salted water for four to five minutes till tender. Drain and refresh in ice-cold water.

Cut the asparagus into short lengths and halve them lengthways. Scrub and thinly slice the carrots. Melt the butter in a non-stick frying pan, pour in a couple of tablespoons of olive oil, then add the asparagus, broad beans and carrots and cook over a moderate to low heat for five minutes.

Chop the chervil or parsley. Break the eggs into a bowl and beat them lightly, just enough to break up the yolks and whites, then add the chopped herbs, some salt and black pepper, and pour into the pan over the asparagus, broad beans and carrots. Keeping the heat low, let the eggs cook till pale gold and slightly set on the base.

Warm an overhead grill. Dust the top of the egg and vegetables with the grated Parmesan, then slide the pan under the heat and leave for a few minutes until the egg mixture is lightly set. Slice in two and serve.

• Cook the vegetables lightly so they retain their spring freshness. If you like your asparagus soft, then boil briefly and drain before adding to the pan. Early peas would make a delightful alternative to the broad beans.

(continued)

• You could, should you wish, incorporate 125g of goat's cheese, broken into small nuggets, into the egg mixture. Swap the vegetables around as you wish, using blanched and chopped spinach or spring cabbage or doubling up on the asparagus. If chervil escapes you, use basil or tarragon. I rather like this with a few garlic leaves in too, roughly chopped and lightly cooked in a little butter.

In a pan   55

AUBERGINE, HONEY, SHEEP'S CHEESE

High summer. Honey bees and thyme.

Serves 2

aubergines, small, slim 6 (about 400g)	lemon thyme leaves 3 tablespoons
sea salt 1 tablespoon	olive oil, for frying
plain flour 5 tablespoons	sheep or goats' cheese 200g
	honey 2 tablespoons

Cut the aubergines lengthways into 1cm-thick slices. Put them in a colander and sprinkle the salt over them, then leave for at least half an hour.

Put the plain flour on a plate and season it with salt and ground black pepper. Finely chop the lemon thyme leaves and stir into the flour. Pat the aubergines dry, then, one by one, put them in the seasoned flour and press them down firmly so the flour sticks to the outside. Then turn and lightly coat the other side. Repeat with all of the slices of aubergine.

Warm a shallow layer of olive oil in a frying pan, then lower in the aubergine slices in a single layer (you may need to do this in batches), and let them cook for three to four minutes until golden. Turn carefully, adding more oil if necessary, and brown the other side. They should be lightly crisp.

Remove the aubergines from the pan and drain briefly on kitchen paper. Transfer to a warm serving dish. Break the cheese into large pieces and scatter among the aubergines. Trickle the honey across the surface and serve while still hot.

• Salting the aubergines simply allows their flesh to relax, and they will soak up less oil as they cook. Get the oil really quite hot before you add them, so they crisp effectively.

• There is a special affinity between aubergines, sheep's cheese and honey, but courgettes work nicely here, too. There is no need to salt them first. You could use hummus instead of the cheese, or a cucumber tzatziki.

COURGETTE (OR MARROW), ZA'ATAR, HERB YOGHURT

Warm spice. Cool sauce.

Serves 2

courgettes (or marrow) 250g
potatoes 350g
an egg
plain flour 1 tablespoon
za'atar 2 heaped teaspoons
small mint leaves 20,
    roughly chopped
a lemon

olive oil, for frying

For the yoghurt:
natural yoghurt 6 tablespoons
chopped parsley 3 tablespoons
chopped mint leaves 1 tablespoon
pomegranate molasses

Grate the courgettes and potatoes, unpeeled, coarsely. Squeeze firmly to remove excess moisture, then place in a mixing bowl with the lightly beaten egg, flour, za'atar and mint leaves. Finely grate the lemon zest and stir in. Salt lightly.

Warm a thin film of oil in a pan that doesn't stick. Shape the mixture into six thick cakes the diameter of a digestive biscuit, squeezing them out between your hands as you go (don't fail to do this), then lower them into the pan. Leave for six minutes or so, until the underside is golden brown, then turn them over carefully and continue till both sides are lightly crisp.

Mix together the yoghurt, parsley and mint leaves. Plate the cakes as soon as they are ready, spoon over the herbed yoghurt, and finish with a trickle of pomegranate molasses.

• Introduce a little chopped red chilli to the herb yoghurt if you like.
• Leave the fritters to crisp lightly on the underside before turning or moving in the pan.

COURGETTES, DILL, CHICKPEAS

Light, crisp fritters. Garlicky chickpea sauce.

Serves 2

cornflour 4 tablespoons
eggs 2
coarse breadcrumbs 100g
chickpeas 2 × 400g cans
garlic 1 clove
olive oil

juice of a small lemon
tahini 1 tablespoon
dill a handful
courgettes 250g
groundnut or vegetable oil, for
        deep frying

Place the cornflour on a plate. Beat the eggs in a shallow dish and tip the breadcrumbs onto a plate.

Drain the chickpeas, then tip them into the bowl of a food processor. Peel and add the garlic, then process to a smooth, soft paste with six tablespoons of olive oil. Stir in the lemon juice, the tahini and the dill. Process briefly.

Slice the courgettes lengthways into large finger-sized batons. Warm enough groundnut or vegetable oil to deep-fry the courgettes, and roll them first in the cornflour, then the beaten egg and lastly the breadcrumbs. As the oil becomes hot enough, lower the courgettes, a few a time, into the oil and let them fry for three or four minutes till crisp outside and soft within. Drain on kitchen paper and serve with the dill hummus.

• If your oil is too hot, the crumbs will cook before the courgette inside is tender. Test the heat of the oil with a small cube of bread. If it turns golden within thirty seconds the oil is too hot. Your courgettes need a good three or four minutes to cook.
• You could use a tempura batter instead of breadcrumbs (80g plain flour and 20g cornflour to 175ml ice-cold water), or serve the hot fritters with a garlic mayonnaise or cucumber tzatziki.

COURGETTES, MUSHROOMS

Late summer. The first hint of autumn.

Serves 2

shallots 250g	assorted mushrooms 350g
butter 50g	basil 16 leaves, torn
olive oil 2 tablespoons	parsley leaves 2 tablespoons, torn
courgettes 150g	half a lemon

Trim the shallots and halve them lengthways, then remove the root of each and separate the layers by teasing them apart. Warm the butter and olive oil in a wide, shallow pan, then sauté the shallots for ten minutes, turning them occasionally until they are lightly coloured.

Halve the courgettes lengthways, then lower them into the pan and let them cook for five to six minutes until they are lightly golden and tender. Remove the shallots and courgettes from the pan and keep warm.

Sort and check the mushrooms (*see below*), then put them in the pan and fry for two or three minutes until golden. Return the courgettes and shallots to the pan and continue cooking until hot, then stir in the basil, parsley and a squeeze of lemon juice. Check the seasoning and serve.

• Use any mushrooms for this, including chestnut and button varieties, but the dish is more interesting if you mix things up a little. The mushrooms need to be added in a specific order if their textures are to be preserved. The tougher varieties such as chestnut and king oyster should be thickly sliced and added first, followed by the softer-textured. Last of all, introduce the most fragile – the tiny shimeji or other small, tender mushrooms. The last ones need only five or six minutes in the pan.

• The mushrooms and courgettes here make a fine, rustic pasta sauce. Cook flat ribbon pasta such as pappardelle in deep, generously salted boiling water till tender, then drain and toss with the mushrooms and courgettes above.

AUBERGINE, CHILLI, SOY

Crisp aubergines. Hot, sweet chilli sauce.

Serves 2

an egg
iced water 4 tablespoons
plain flour 2 tablespoons
soft brown sugar 30g
rice vinegar 3 tablespoons
light soy sauce 2 tablespoons
chilli paste 2 tablespoons

sesame seeds 2 tablespoons
aubergines 400g
sunflower, groundnut or
    vegetable oil 250ml
a few coriander leaves
a small hot, red chilli

Whisk together the egg, water and flour. Salt it lightly and set aside.

Put the brown sugar in a small saucepan with the vinegar, soy sauce and chilli paste. Bring to the boil, then remove from the heat and put to one side. Tip the sesame seeds into a small, shallow pan and toast over a moderate heat until fragrant and walnut brown. Remove the pan from the heat.

Slice each aubergine in half lengthways and then into six segments. Heat the oil in a small, deep pan, then, when it is thoroughly hot, dip the aubergine pieces in the batter and add them carefully to the oil. Cook for five minutes or until the outer batter is crisp, the inner flesh soft as marshmallow.

Drain each piece of aubergine briefly on kitchen paper then trickle over the chilli sauce, sprinkle with some of the sesame seeds, and serve with a little coriander for those who like it, and perhaps a small, ripe chilli, sliced as thin as tissue paper.

• I use small aubergines, the size of a duck egg, for this. They tend to live in Middle Eastern and Asian greengrocers. The heat of the oil is important, being hot enough to set the thin batter but not so hot it burns before the flesh is cooked. About 160°C is fine.

FENNEL, ONIONS, EGGS

Tender vegetables and a runny egg.

Serves 2

2 large carrots	butter a thin slice
fennel a large bulb or 3 small	yellow mustard seeds 1 teaspoon
a medium onion	eggs 2
olive oil	

Scrub the carrots, then slice into short lengths, about the size of a wine cork. Cook them in deep boiling water for ten minutes or until soft to the point of a knife. Drain and set aside.

Cut the fennel into quarters lengthways. Peel the onion, then cut in half and slice each half into four segments. Warm a couple of tablespoons of olive oil in a large frying pan over a moderately high heat, then add the butter. When it has melted, add the onion and fennel and leave to colour lightly. An occasional stir will help them cook evenly.

Add the carrots to the onion and fennel, stir in the mustard seeds and continue to cook for a further five minutes until the carrots are golden here and there. Season with salt and black pepper.

When all is golden and sizzling, transfer to two warm plates. Return the pan to the heat and add a shallow film of olive oil or butter. Break in the eggs and fry till they are how you like them. Lift the eggs from the pan with a fish slice and add one to the top of each of the plates of vegetables.

• Chop and change the vegetables to suit what you have to hand – this is very much a fridge-tidy fry-up – but the balance is important. The fennel is there as a contrast to the sweetness of the carrots, but celery would work too, as would asparagus. The vegetables should be cooked till tender but slightly crisper than the carrot. The dish is best with a contrast of textures. The egg provides an instant 'sauce' to bring it together.

(continued)

• You could use boiled and sliced potatoes instead of carrots and asparagus, cooked whole, instead of the fennel. You could include broad beans, lightly steamed, and young beetroot if you wish. A poached or soft-boiled egg would be a good alternative to the fried egg. As would a slice of soft, buttery cheese to melt over the vegetables.

PASTA, TOMATOES

Hot, cold, crisp, tender. A dish of contrasts. A fideuà salad.

Serves 4

garlic 2 cloves
olive oil 3 tablespoons
vegetable stock 1 litre
small pasta shapes *(see overleaf)* 250g

tomatoes 4 medium
cherry tomatoes 300g
parsley a handful
spring onions 4

You will need a heavy-based frying pan or paella pan.

Peel and thinly slice the garlic. Warm the oil in a large sauté pan, then add the garlic and cook till just starting to crisp. Meanwhile, heat the stock in a separate pan. Tip the pasta into the garlic and sauté for one minute, then pour in the hot stock and bring to the boil.

Lower the heat to a simmer, then cover with a lid and cook for ten minutes until the pasta is almost tender. Remove the lid and continue to simmer for a further ten minutes, until the liquid has almost all evaporated. The pasta should be starting to toast lightly on the base of the pan. If it isn't, pour in a drop or two more oil.

Cut the bigger tomatoes into quarters and the cherry tomatoes in half, then roughly chop the parsley and spring onions. Use a wooden spatula to scrape the toasted pasta from the bottom of the pan, ensuring all the golden crusty bits come with it. Tip in all the tomatoes, parsley and onions and toss together gently so the cold tomatoes, hot pasta and small amount of stock are thoroughly mixed. Check the seasoning and serve.

• The trick is to catch the pasta just at the point where it is starting to crisp on the bottom of the pan and can be loosened with the end of a wooden spatula. The point here is the contrast between hot and cold, soft and crisp. It may need a little practice, but is very pleasing, and certainly the best pasta salad I have ever had. *(continued)*

• Ideas about the correct pasta to use for fideuà will be argued about even in Spain, but the only really essential point is to use a small, thin pasta that will crisp nicely on the bottom of the pan. There are several suitable types – fideos, vermicelli or angel hair would all be good. You could even break thin noodles into short lengths.

GNOCCHI, TOMATO, RADISHES

Hot, crisp and chewy gnocchi. A crunchy, refreshing salsa.

Serves 2–3

ready-made gnocchi 500g	parsley a small handful
assorted tomatoes 400g	garlic 2 cloves
radishes 8	olive oil 3 tablespoons
spring onions 4	butter 40g

Bring a deep pan of salted water to the boil. When the water is bubbling furiously, add the gnocchi. Let them cook until each little dumpling has risen to the surface. Remove with a slotted spoon and drain them in a colander.

Dice the tomatoes and put them in a bowl. Slice the radishes and finely chop the spring onions. Finely chop the parsley leaves. Mix the tomatoes, radishes, onions and parsley together and chill.

Peel the garlic cloves and slice them finely. Warm the olive oil in a shallow pan, then add the butter and let it melt. Put the garlic into the oil and butter. Keep the heat low and add the drained gnocchi. Let the garlic and gnocchi cook for a good ten minutes until the outside of each little dumpling is golden and lightly crisp. The garlic should be a deep walnut brown in colour. Remove the gnocchi to a serving dish, then add the garlic and diced tomatoes, radishes, onion and parsley and toss gently together.

• The texture of the cooked gnocchi is at its most pleasing when the outside is crisp and the inside fudgy. The dumplings need to be watched carefully as they fry, turning them with kitchen tongs now and again so they crisp evenly. They should be a deep nutty gold when cooked. The contrast of the hot, soft dumplings with the crisp chilled tomato is best when the salad is thoroughly chilled before tossing with the piping hot gnocchi. *(continued)*

• For a cooler day, let the tomatoes cook for fifteen minutes with a little olive oil, so they soften into an impromptu sauce. Add a splash of red wine vinegar as they approach softness. Toss the hot gnocchi in the sauce at the very last minute so they retain some of their crispness.

HALLOUMI, MINT, AUBERGINE

Smoky flavours. Silky aubergine. Crisp crumbs.

Serves 2

aubergines, medium 2
half a whole head of garlic
olive oil
half a lemon
dried breadcrumbs 100g
dried thyme 2 tablespoons

eggs 2
half a pomegranate
halloumi 250g
sunflower or groundnut oil, for frying
small mint leaves a handful

Set the oven at 220°C/Gas 7. Place the aubergines and the half head of garlic (about six cloves) in a roasting tin and bake for about forty-five minutes, until the skin of the aubergines is black and the flesh is soft.

Remove the tin from the oven, slice the aubergines in half and scrape out the flesh with a spoon, discarding the skins as you go. Roughly chop or mash the flesh and place in a mixing bowl. Separate the garlic cloves, then squeeze into the bowl, discarding their skins. Beat in a couple of tablespoons of olive oil. Squeeze in the lemon juice, a tablespoon at a time, tasting as you go, then season with a little salt and set aside.

Place the breadcrumbs on a plate, then mix in the thyme and a few twists of ground black pepper. Break the eggs into a small dish and beat lightly with a fork to combine yolks and whites. Separate the seeds from the pomegranate. Cut the halloumi into thick fingers.

Roll the halloumi first in the beaten egg, then in the seasoned crumbs, and place on a plate. Warm a thin layer of olive or groundnut oil in a shallow pan, lower in the halloumi, a few fingers at a time, and fry for a minute or two till crisp, then rest them briefly on kitchen paper.

Divide the creamed aubergine between two plates, then add the crisp halloumi, a scattering of the pomegranate seeds and a handful of small mint leaves.   *(continued)*

• The aubergine needs to be baked until it is truly soft – it will have collapsed – and the flesh can be crushed effortlessly with a fork. The halloumi, once fried, should be eaten immediately, as the crumb crust needs to be crisp to be good.

• You might like to bake the halloumi instead of frying it. Slice the block of cheese in half horizontally, then place in a large sheet of kitchen foil. Pour over a glug of oil, add some black pepper and dried thyme, scrunch the foil loosely to seal, and bake for twenty minutes at 200°C/Gas 6.

MARROW, TOMATO, COUSCOUS

A taste of late summer.

Serves 2–3

marrow 600g	golden sultanas 3 tablespoons
tomatoes 750g	couscous 60g
garlic 2 cloves	parsley 30g
olive oil	pumpkin seeds 2 tablespoons
tarragon 6 sprigs	

Peel the marrow, cut it in half lengthways and discard all the pith and seeds. Cut into thick pieces about 2cm in width. Roughly chop the tomatoes. Peel and slice the garlic. Warm two tablespoons of oil in a pan, add the marrow, tomatoes and garlic and leave to simmer for about twenty minutes. Tear the leaves from the tarragon and stir them in. After about fifteen minutes' cooking, when all is tender and on the point of collapse, stir in the sultanas, then season generously with salt and black pepper.

While the tomato and marrow mixture is cooking, soak the couscous in enough hot water to cover it. The couscous will swell and soak up the water. Chop the leaves from the parsley, discarding the stalks. Roughly chop the pumpkin seeds and stir them through the couscous together with the parsley. When the tomato and marrow stew is tender and juicy, check the seasoning and serve in shallow bowls with the pumpkin seed and parsley couscous.

• This is one of those dishes at its best when allowed to simmer to an almost soupy softness. Watch the liquid levels as it cooks. If the juices are running low, pour in a little vegetable stock. The sultanas lend a chutney note to this vegetable stew, but the flavours here are herbal rather than spicy, so any herbs you have to hand – tarragon, basil, lemon thyme – are all sound additions. *(continued)*

• You could use courgettes in place of the marrow. Simply cut each one in half and then into short lengths. Tarragon and basil are my herbs of choice with marrow, but lemon thyme is a winner, too. I like the purity of this dish but, if you wish, add onions at the start, cooked until pale and soft, before you add the tomatoes and marrow. You can add spices, too, such as coriander and cumin seeds, roughly ground.

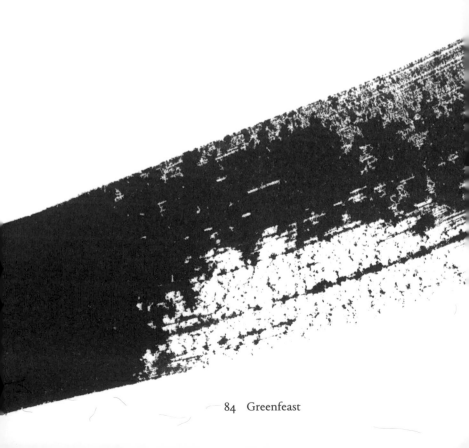

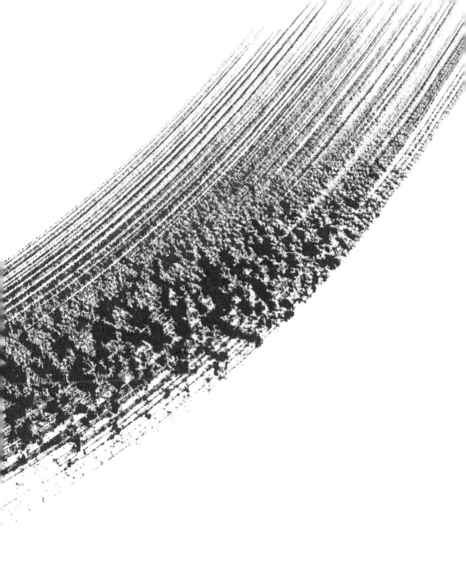

PEAS, BREADCRUMBS

Crunchy fritters. Soft green peas.

Makes 6 fritters, serves 2

frozen peas 500g	*To coat and fry:*
tarragon leaves 20g	eggs 2, beaten
butter 40g	dry white breadcrumbs
egg yolks 2	a couple of large handfuls
dry, white breadcrumbs	butter a thick slice
6 tablespoons	olive or vegetable oil a little

Boil the peas for about four minutes in lightly salted water, then drain them. Leave them in a colander under cold running water until thoroughly chilled, then tip into the bowl of a food processor, add the tarragon and butter and process to a coarse paste. Transfer to a bowl and chill thoroughly. Once chilled, fold the egg yolks and the breadcrumbs into the pea mixture.

Pour the beaten egg into a shallow dish and spread the remaining breadcrumbs on a plate. Shape the pea mixture into six short, fat barrel-shaped croquettes. Roll each croquette in the beaten egg, then in the crumbs, and chill for twenty minutes.

Warm the thick slice of butter and the oil, then fry the croquettes, over a moderate heat, gently rolling them over now and again to colour evenly. Drain, briefly, on kitchen paper and serve.

SPRING CABBAGE, SPRING ONIONS, POTATOES

Humble bubble and squeak. A handful of herbs.

Serves 3

potatoes 500g	butter 40g
spring cabbage 250g	olive oil and a little butter,
spring onions 3	for frying
mint, dill, tarragon, chopped	watercress or pea shoots
8 tablespoons	a handful

Peel and roughly chop the potatoes, then boil in deep, lightly salted water for fifteen to twenty minutes till tender enough to mash.

Remove the core from the spring cabbage and discard it, then roughly chop the leaves. Cook in a saucepan with a little boiling water for eight to ten minutes, then drain thoroughly.

Slice the spring onions finely, discarding any tough dark green leaves as you go.

Drain the potatoes thoroughly, add the butter, then mash them using a food mixer fitted with a flat paddle attachment, or with a potato masher. Fold the spring cabbage, onions and herbs into the potato together with a little ground black pepper.

Roll the mixture into nine balls or thick patties, using a little flour on your hands if necessary.

Warm a thin layer of olive oil and a little butter in a shallow, non-stick pan over a moderate heat, then lower in the patties, letting them cook for five or six minutes till pale gold and lightly crisp on the underside. Turn each one over and brown the other side.

Divide the watercress or pea shoots between three plates, and add the sizzling patties. *(continued)*

• Traditionally, bubble and squeak was a way to use up leftover vegetables from the Sunday roast, but I think it is worth making from scratch, with freshly mashed potatoes and crisp spring greens. Make sure to drain the potatoes thoroughly, to avoid a wet mash. Wring the greens lightly in your fist – this is important – to squeeze out any excess water.

• I like this made with pale green, early summer cabbage, but try cavolo nero or tenderstem broccoli too. The mixture of herbs is up to you. Parsley is a must, but any soft-stemmed herbs can be used. Avoid thyme, sage and rosemary here and go for the tender herbs such as tarragon, mint, fennel fronds and dill.

SWEET POTATOES, TOMATOES

Glowing cakes. The piquancy of tomatoes.

Serves 2

sweet potatoes 1kg
butter 50g
dried, fine breadcrumbs 120g
lemon zest, finely grated
　　1 teaspoon
tarragon leaves, chopped
　　1 tablespoon
an egg
a little flour

groundnut or vegetable oil,
　　for shallow frying

For the quick tomato sauce:
tomatoes 500g
garlic 2 cloves
olive oil 3 tablespoons
basil leaves 10

Peel the sweet potatoes and cut into large chunks, then steam for about twenty minutes till tender enough to crush. Mash with the butter and set aside to cool.

Put the breadcrumbs on a plate, then add the zest and tarragon and combine. Crack the egg into a shallow bowl and briefly beat with a fork to mix the white and yolk.

When the mash is cool, shape into four large balls and pat them, with floury hands, into patties. Dip the patties first into the beaten egg, then into the crumbs. Put them on a baking sheet and refrigerate for thirty minutes.

Make the tomato sauce: chop the tomatoes. Crush the garlic. Warm the olive oil in a saucepan, add the tomatoes and garlic and a little salt and simmer for fifteen to twenty minutes, stirring regularly. Tear and stir in the basil, and season with black pepper.

Warm a little groundnut or vegetable oil in a non-stick frying pan, then lower the cakes into the hot oil and leave to cook, without moving

(continued)

them, for four or five minutes until the underside is crisp and golden. Carefully, using a palette knife or fish slice, turn the cakes over and lightly crisp the other side. Serve with the tomato and basil sauce.

• Drain the potatoes very thoroughly before mashing. Let the mash cool before shaping and allow the cakes to rest fully before cooking. If your mixture seems too soft to shape, stir in a tablespoon or two of flour. Once you have put the cakes into the hot oil, don't move them until the base has crisped, turn them carefully over and let the other side become completely crisp before removing from the pan.

In a pan   95

IN THE HAND

Nothing comes close to a bacon sandwich made with white bread. No matter, there are myriad meatless possibilities to embrace. Dark, treacly rye bread with a dill-flecked cottage cheese, acid-sweet pink pickled onions and crisp cucumber; soft, thickly-cut sourdough with avocado, capers and a mayonnaise with chopped parsley, rocket, tarragon; and flatbread, warm from the griddle, stuffed with crushed, roasted aubergine, mint and crumbled sheep's cheese or a bland and chewy bagel with mozzarella, onion and a mustard-seeded guacamole.

The soft, flour- or cornmeal-dusted bun begs for a crisp filling, perhaps of a sizzling patty of grated carrot, Parmesan and radishes and garlic mayonnaise or asparagus that you have fried tempura-style and slathered with lemon mayonnaise. The giving, daisy-fresh softness of the bun is the most suitable vehicle for coins of courgette fried till crisp and tossed in a ricotta and mint dressing, or perhaps you might like to think about grilled halloumi and slivers of artichokes from a jar.

Let us delve further into the contrast of crisp bread and soft fillings. Imagine toasted white bread with melting cheese, cornichons and capers (I do think you should have both); a seeded Scandinavian-style crispbread with grated celeriac, beetroot and pickled cucumbers in a mustard dressing; sea salt and rosemary-encrusted focaccia sandwiched with sliced preserved artichokes, shavings of Parmesan and a trickle of olive oil.

A sandwich doesn't need a lid, though we use one to keep our fingers clean. But some possibilities are past such pedestrian concerns. Grilled slices of baguette topped with grilled tomatoes brushed with thyme leaves and crushed garlic; a mustardy Welsh rarebit cut into bite-sized pieces and served with a tiny, icy beer; panettone with hot, fried apples and a thick wave of crème fraîche.

Food eaten in the hand is, as a general rule, emergency in nature. We don't often plan what to stick between two pieces of bread for immediate gratification. Perhaps we should. Just because we are eschewing knives and forks doesn't necessarily mean our meal should be thrown together with little care or thought. Get a sandwich right and it will satiate as successfully as anything on a plate. Especially if we have considered the textures.

Picture two slices of soft white bread filled with hummus. Doesn't really work, does it? But toast that bread or, better still, sandwich the filling between a duo of warm, sesame-freckled pieces of flatbread and you have a feast. A tempura-fried aubergine caught between two pieces of crispbread is almost a chore to eat, yet stuff it into a soft bun, add a dollop of yoghurt and you have seriously good food in your hand. We shouldn't abandon our usual ability to match hot with cold, soft with crunchy, spicy with comfortingly bland just because we are making something that will never see a tablecloth.

CARROTS, TOMATOES, BUNS

Soft buns. Crisp carrots. A crunchy salsa.

Makes 4

large carrots 325g

spring onions 3

eggs 2

plain flour 1 tablespoon

grated Parmesan 3 heaped
tablespoons

garlic mayonnaise 4 tablespoons

groundnut oil 3 tablespoons

large soft buns 4

For the salsa:

tomatoes 3 medium

radishes 6

coriander leaves a handful

olive oil 2 tablespoons

balsamic vinegar 2 teaspoons

Peel or scrub the carrots, then grate them coarsely. (The coarse grater attachment of a food processor works well for me.) Finely slice the spring onions and add them to the carrots. Lightly beat the eggs, then fold into the carrot mixture followed by the flour and grated Parmesan.

Shape the mixture into eight shallow patties roughly the diameter of a digestive biscuit, placing them on a baking sheet as you go. Refrigerate for twenty minutes to firm them up.

Slice the tomatoes thinly and put them into a bowl. Halve the radishes from root to tip and toss with the tomatoes, half the torn coriander leaves, the oil and vinegar and a little salt. Chop the remaining coriander and stir into the mayonnaise.

Warm the groundnut oil in a shallow non-stick pan, then lower the patties into the oil, letting them fry till golden. Using a palette knife or fish slice, turn them over and lightly brown the other side. They are fragile, so turn in one swift, confident move to prevent them breaking.

Split the buns horizontally and toast lightly on their cut sides. Spoon a little of the tomato and radish mixture on the base of each bun, followed

(continued)

by a carrot patty, a few more tomatoes, then another patty and the herb and garlic mayonnaise. Place the lids on the buns and serve.

• I like to make crisp, loose tangles of carrot and spring onion to fill soft, warm bread. The small amount of flour in the recipe means they are fragile and need turning with care if they are not to break up. (That said, I don't mind if they do, the little nuggets crisping appetisingly in the pan.) The alternative is to add more flour, which I think destroys their delicate nature. A tomato and coriander salsa, kept coarse, makes them sing.

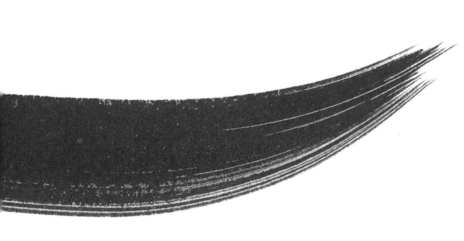

In the hand   103

FETA, BEETROOT, BUNS

Soft buns. Cool mint. Salty feta. Peppery rocket and crisp beetroot.

Makes 2 buns

feta 200g
olive oil
raw beetroots 2 small
white wine vinegar 1 tablespoon
mint leaves 6

natural yoghurt 100g
large soft buns 2
pea shoots a small handful
rocket a handful

Warm a griddle pan. Slice the block of feta in half horizontally to give two rectangular slabs. Brush them with olive oil, then place on the hot griddle and leave to brown lightly. Turn and brown the other side. Remove and set aside.

While the feta is on the griddle, peel and coarsely grate the beetroots into a bowl. Season lightly with salt and black pepper, then add the vinegar and toss to coat. Shred the mint and add to the beetroot together with the yoghurt. Fold together.

Split the buns and toast them on the cut sides. Spread the bottom halves with a little of the mint yoghurt from the beetroot, add the pea shoots and rocket, then place the feta on top. Add a generous amount of the beetroot, cover with the other bun halves and serve with any remaining beetroot.

MUSTARD GUACAMOLE, MOZZARELLA, BAGEL

A rough textured avocado cream. Mustard's gentle heat.

Makes 4

a red onion
white wine vinegar 100ml
avocados 2
grain mustard 2 teaspoons
coriander leaves a small handful

juice of half a lemon
olive oil 1 tablespoon
bagels 4
mozzarella 1 × 200g ball

Peel the onion and slice into 5mm-thick rings, then put them into a small pan with enough water to cover and add the vinegar. Bring to the boil, then remove from the heat, cover with a lid and set aside for ten minutes.

Halve, stone and peel the avocados, put the flesh in a bowl, then crush it with a fork. Stir in the mustard, coriander and lemon juice, then fold in the olive oil to give a textured, mustard-seed-freckled cream.

Split the bagels in half and spread the bottom half of each generously with the avocado cream. Tear the mozzarella into large, irregular pieces and place on top of the avocado, then add several rings of drained pickled pink onion to each. Place the other bagel half on top and serve.

• A surprisingly substantial sandwich, and one that requires a couple of perfect avocados. Not just à point, but unblemished. A sandwich to be eaten within minutes of the avocado being crushed.

IN THE
MORNING

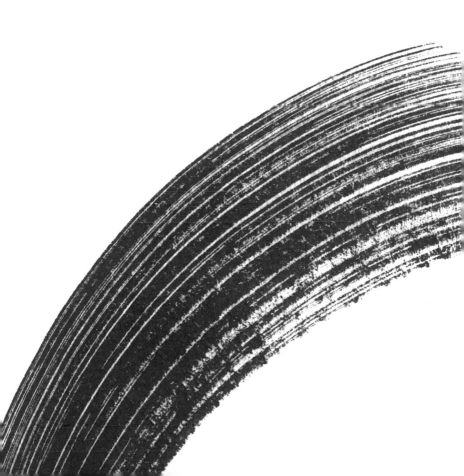

I wake hungry. The need for something to eat is invariably what gets me out of bed. A bowl of porridge in winter, one of chilled Bircher muesli in spring. Summer is rarely anything more substantial than fruit – watermelon or cantaloupe – cold from the fridge.

The choices for breakfast are easier in spring and summer. We don't need to think about stoking ourselves up to fight the cold weather before we leave for work. A smoothie, possibly of mango or blueberry, is made in seconds in a blender with yoghurt, ice and a few leaves of fresh mint. I like to make a mango or raspberry smoothie on the thick side with the addition of a banana, scoop the silky purée into a bowl, then sprinkle the surface with pumpkin and sunflower seeds, flaked almonds, toasted rolled oats and linseeds. The latter given a quick ride in the spice grinder to break them up.

To what I call 'smoothie bowls' you can add anything from nori flakes to whole berries, chia seeds to toasted nuts. I would suggest that you don't overload them though. It is all too easy to add one ingredient too many.

To those brought up on a full English, the idea of vegetables, at least green ones, may seem plain wrong for breakfast, but I like them. An avocado of course, sliced in half, stone removed, peeled, then sliced into wedges. The green, buttery flesh is flattered by the addition of pink grapefruit. Avocado on toast may have passed into ubiquity now, but it is still a fine yet gentle start to the day. Some add a shake of chilli sauce or a pebbledash of sunflower seeds. Others might opt for a poached egg. For others, the avocado is simply a jumping-off point, something to add to a smoothie of other green things, kale, watercress and the like, but that treads slightly too far into eating for health rather than enjoyment for me. It's a narrow line but one on which I know where I stand.

I have eaten yoghurt every day for as long as I can remember. The cool, lactic sharpness seems particularly suited to early morning, and I often take it unsullied, in a small china bowl. A scattering of blueberries, blackberries or a swirl of blackcurrant compote is the only further attention its pure white surface gets.

It is but a short step from yoghurt to soft cheese. The breakfast habits I picked up while filming in the Middle East have stayed with me, and at least two morning feasts a week will involve flatbread, soft, sharp cheese and a sweet-sour preserve. The flatbread must be warm. The cheese should have the piercing sharpness of sheep's milk. The jam is best when cherry, quince or apricot. Otherwise the effect will be too sweet.

Bircher muesli, the mixture of yoghurt, oats and fruits, has the advantage of being light but also deeply sustaining. I do insist on the soaked oats, yoghurt and grated apple of the classic recipe being served well chilled, and I tend to leave the raisins on the shelf. I want bright, clean flavours early in the day, so stoned cherries, sliced strawberries, raspberries or blueberries replace the dried fruits so beloved of Dr Bircher. I update it too with a sprinkling of chia and linseeds, and a little pinhead oatmeal toasted till it smells nutty.

Little cakes of ricotta are a splendid late weekend breakfast. I make a thick batter from egg yolks folded into ricotta with a handful of dark berries, a little flour or cornmeal, then lighten it with beaten egg white. The result can be cooked in a non-stick pan, in little puddles the size of a biscuit and fried till soft and golden. You can gild the lily with a spoonful of honey or a dusting of icing sugar and more berries.

If warm flatbreads and hot ricotta cakes, smoothies and chilled oat porridges are not your thing, you might like to take the miso soup route. Hot soup made with white miso paste is a breakfast I never tire of. A deeply savoury yet light soup, taken as it comes or with the addition of a few shredded vegetables, it has one of the most comforting smells. I use a commercial soup mix but you can easily make your own. For each person put two heaped table-spoons of white miso paste (I rather like a half-and-half mixture of white and brown) into a deep bowl, pour in 200ml of dashi stock and stir thoroughly until the miso paste has melted. You can drink as it is, or introduce some ground, toasted sesame seeds, or a few cubes of soft tofu.

In the morning 113

STRAWBERRIES, OATS, YOGHURT

A bowl of early morning calm.

Serves 4–6

porridge oats 100g
rolled jumbo oats 50g
apple juice 400ml
honey 2 teaspoons
strawberries 250g
caster sugar 2 tablespoons,
    plus a little extra

juice of half an orange
balsamic vinegar a drop or two
an apple
natural yoghurt 100g

Sprinkle the oats in a single layer over the surface of a large shallow pan and toast them lightly over a moderate heat. Remove from the heat when they smell warm and nutty and their colour has darkened slightly.

Let the oats cool, then put them in a bowl with the apple juice, honey, a little sugar if you wish and a generous pinch of salt. Cover and refrigerate overnight.

Slice the strawberries, put them in a mixing bowl and scatter the sugar over them. Add the orange juice, then add a few drops of balsamic vinegar to taste. Set aside in the fridge overnight.

Next morning, coarsely grate the apple and fold into the Bircher muesli with the yoghurt, followed by the strawberries, then serve.

• Dr Bircher's classic muesli is one of my favourite breakfasts, though I will admit to removing the raisins, which I find introduce an unwelcome sweetness. This is a fresher version, with sliced strawberries and orange.
• In my book, Bircher muesli only really works if it is served thoroughly chilled. The overnight process is necessary not only for the oats to swell, but for the ingredients to become totally cold.

IN THE OVEN

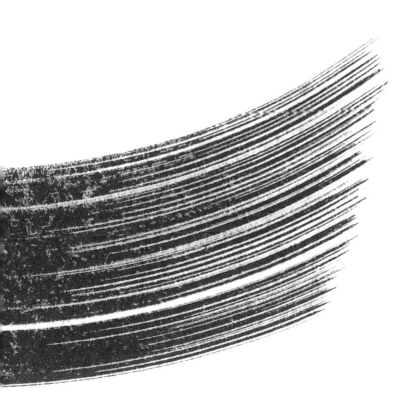

There is a summer dinner I turn to when I really can't be bothered to cook. And yes, that does actually happen after a long, hot day. My dinner involves switching on the oven, putting four field mushrooms in a roasting tin, sloshing over some olive oil, butter, salt and pepper, a squeeze of lemon followed by the empty lemon shells and a handful of thyme branches, then I leave it in the oven for forty minutes or so. What emerges are dark, herb-flecked mushrooms, scented with pepper, lemon and thyme. The copious and surprisingly aromatic juices are mopped up with bread. I wipe the rest up from my plate with a few leaves of pale, soft lettuce. The dish involves ten minutes' preparation, if that. The smell is pure summer, the flavours gentle, the whole dish light and fresh.

There is a notion that anything cooked in the oven is winter fare. Baking, roasting, pastry-topped dishes, a crisp-skinned potato perhaps, a slow braise of long-cooked flavours. But I do use the oven in summer too. A summer gratin of pasta, cheese and a sauce made from cream and young kale fits the bill nicely. I bake new potatoes in their skins till crisp, then serve with a pesto of basil and Pecorino or fresh goat's cheese into which I have folded shredded basil and mint leaves. I am exceptionally fond of baked aubergines that, once ready, I spread with a mixture of white miso and honey and return, briefly, to the heat.

There are vegetable tarts for eating in summer – rectangles of puff pastry laden with creamed aubergines and pine kernels, but there are others too: a sheet of puff pastry spread with pesto, a layer of sliced tomatoes, then a trickle of olive oil; another sheet of pastry baked unfilled, then, as it emerges golden from the oven, topped with ricotta cheese, crushed peas, mint and grated lemon zest. Or simply spread the pastry with cream cheese and cover with asparagus spears and grated Parmesan.

An infinitely useful dish for the summer is a roasting tin's worth of peppers, red, orange, yellow perhaps, roasted with a splash of olive oil till they collapse and their skins turn black. Peeled and dressed with olive oil they will keep for several days and can be sliced and fried with artichoke hearts, green beans or thin slices of summer squash. You can use the soft-fleshed peppers as a base and spoon hummus and bean purées on top, or stuff with soft, sharp cheeses and herbs. Courgettes can be roasted too, then reheated as and when needed, for tossing with pappardelle, basil, pine kernels and lemon.

ASPARAGUS, PUFF PASTRY

Six little tarts, light as a summer breeze.

Makes 6 small tarts

asparagus 8 spears
puff pastry 250g
an egg, beaten

goat's cheese 150g
cream cheese 150g
fresh thyme leaves a teaspoon

Set the oven at 200°C/Gas 6. Put an upturned baking sheet in the oven. Bring a medium pan of water to the boil. Trim the asparagus, then cut each spear into three short lengths. Drop the asparagus into the pan and let it boil for two minutes, before lifting out with a slotted spoon and refreshing in iced water.

Roll the pastry out to a rectangle measuring 34 × 22 cm. Cut the rectangle into six equal squares. Place the squares on a lined baking sheet. Using the tip of a knife, score a square 1cm inside each. Brush a little beaten egg around the outside square of each pastry.

Drain the asparagus on kitchen paper. Crush the goat's cheese with a fork and fold in the cream cheese and thyme. Divide the mixture between the six squares of pastry and put four asparagus pieces on each. Put the baking sheet on top of the preheated sheet already in the oven, and bake for twenty-five to thirty minutes, until the tarts are golden. Eat immediately.

• I reckon on two of these little tarts per portion. Perhaps a grain salad on the side.

AUBERGINE, HAZELNUTS, ONIONS

The contrast of silky aubergine with crunchy, toasted hazelnuts.

Serves 3

aubergines 3	olive oil 6 tablespoons
onions, medium 2	hazelnuts 100g
a head of garlic	parsley leaves a handful
rosemary sprigs 5	

Set the oven at 200°C/Gas 6. Slice the aubergines in half lengthways, then put them in a large roasting tin. Peel and halve the onions, cut them into segments, then add to the tin along with the whole head of garlic. Remove the rosemary needles from their stems and scatter over the aubergines and onions. Douse everything with the olive oil and bake for 45 minutes.

Halve each of the hazelnuts. Remove the aubergines and garlic from the roasting tin, then add the nuts to the tin and roast for five to ten minutes until golden brown.

Squeeze the soft garlic flesh from its skin into a mixing bowl and discard the papery skin. Scrape the flesh from three of the aubergine halves into the bowl and discard the skin. Fold the onions and any roasting juices into the aubergine and check the seasoning.

Scatter the parsley and hazelnuts over the aubergine mixture, then pile onto the reserved halves.

• Pine kernels, toasted, flaked almonds or cashew nuts will offer a welcome crunch instead of hazelnuts should you wish.

AUBERGINE, PUFF PASTRY

Crisp pastry. The softness of roast aubergines.

Serves 2

aubergines 2, about 700g total weight	*For the basil sauce:*
	pine kernels 30g
olive oil	basil leaves and stems 30g
puff pastry 125g	garlic 1 clove
a little beaten egg	olive oil 120ml

Set the oven at 200°C/Gas 6. Slice the aubergines in half lengthways and put them cut side up in a roasting tin. Score the cut surface of the aubergines first one way, then the other, cutting almost through to the skin. Trickle a tablespoon or so of olive oil over each one, letting it seep down into the cuts.

Grind a little salt and black pepper over the aubergines, then bake for almost an hour till the surface is golden brown and the insides are soft and silky.

On a floured board, roll the pastry out into a rectangle measuring 26 × 15cm. Place the pastry on a lined baking sheet and score a line along each side of the pastry to form a 1cm-wide rim. Try not to cut right through the pastry. Brush the rim of pastry with a little beaten egg, then refrigerate for thirty minutes.

Remove the aubergines from the oven, then scoop the flesh into a bowl. Discard the skins and reserve the oil and cooking juices in the tin. Place the chilled pastry in the oven and bake for ten to twelve minutes until risen and pale gold in colour.

Toast the pine kernels in a dry, shallow pan. Put the basil and garlic into the bowl of a food processor, add two-thirds of the pine kernels, then pour in the oil and cooking juices from the aubergine and blend to a rough purée. Roughly break up the aubergine with a spoon or fork, then fold in the basil paste. *(continued)*

Remove the tart case from the oven. Using the back of a teaspoon, press down the scored inner rectangle of pastry to give a hollow, fill with the aubergine mixture, scatter over the reserved pine kernels, then return to the oven for eight to ten minutes till hot. Cut into two and serve.

• The tart gets only a few minutes in the oven, so it is important to make sure the aubergines are thoroughly tender, almost collapsing, before you take them from the oven.

• I sometimes include feta for its affinity to aubergines and oil, but you could also substitute grated Parmesan to introduce a deeper, more savoury note if there is some handy.

HALLOUMI, TOMATOES

Mediterranean flavours for a hot summer's day.

Serves 2

cherry tomatoes 350g	rosemary 4 sprigs
shallots, medium 4	halloumi 250g
olive oil 4 tablespoons	dried chilli flakes ½ teaspoon
thyme 4 sprigs	

Cut the tomatoes in half and put them in a roasting tin. Peel the shallots, cut them in half lengthways, separate them into layers, then add to the tin. Set the oven at 200°C/Gas 6. Pour half the oil over the shallots and tomatoes, season with pepper and a little salt, and add the thyme and rosemary. Toss the vegetables in the oil and aromatics until everything is coated. Leave a space in the centre of the tin for the parcel of halloumi.

Lay a large square of kitchen foil on a baking sheet. Slice the halloumi in half horizontally. Spoon over the remaining oil and scatter with the chilli flakes. Loosely pull the edges of the foil together to form a parcel, then scrunch the edges together to seal. Place in the middle of the tin.

Bake for 35 minutes until the vegetables are sweet and soft, stirring halfway so the vegetables don't stick to the tin. Divide the vegetables between two plates, open up the parcel and add the halloumi and its juices to the vegetables, then serve.

• Shallots and onions cook much more quickly if the layers are separated. Slice the shallot in half lengthways, then cut off the root and about 1cm of the flesh to make it easier to separate the layers. Baking the cheese in loose foil prevents it from drying out.

• I sometimes add courgettes, thinly sliced, to the tomatoes and onions. You can also fold shredded basil leaves into the vegetables five minutes before they are ready.

BAKED PEPPERS, BEANS, HERB SAUCE

Sweet peppers. Toasted beans. Piquant sauce.

Serves 2

peppers, large 2	cornichons 40g
olive oil 160ml	Dijon mustard 2 teaspoons
basil 20g	sherry vinegar 1 tablespoon
parsley 20g	cannellini beans 1 × 400g can
mint 10g	

Set the oven at 200°C/Gas 6. Place the peppers in a small roasting tin, trickle generously with 60ml of the oil, then bake for twenty-five minutes. Turn them over and cook for another twenty minutes.

Remove the leaves from the herbs. Chop the cornichons. Using a blender, mix together the herb leaves, mustard and the remaining oil. Turn off the machine then stir in the chopped cornichons and the vinegar.

Drain and rinse the beans, then add to the peppers, tossing them in the juices in the roasting tin. Return to the oven to cook for fifteen minutes until the beans are hot and the peppers soft, sweet and blackened.

Serve the peppers and beans with the green sauce.

• For roast peppers to be worth eating it is essential to roast them till their skins are brown, even blackened in patches. Be brave with the heat – the peppers will be sweeter and silkier that way.
• I like the way the beans cook in the roasting tin, becoming almost crunchy, but sometimes I cook them inside the peppers instead. Cut the peppers in half and roast them, fill the halves with a mixture of beans and the dressing and return to the oven.

BAKED RICOTTA, ASPARAGUS

Light, yet not without substance. A homely dish of cheese and eggs.

Serves 2–3

asparagus 300g

ricotta 500g

thyme leaves 1 tablespoon

Parmesan 95g, grated

eggs 2

a little butter for the dish

Set the oven at 200°C/Gas 6. Put a pan of water on to boil. Trim the asparagus, discarding any tough stalks, then cut each spear into short lengths. When the water is boiling, salt it lightly, then add the asparagus and cook for two or three minutes. Drain and set aside.

Put the ricotta in a mixing bowl and add the thyme leaves. Add most of the grated Parmesan, then most of the drained asparagus, reserving a few of the loveliest spears for the top. Break the eggs into a small bowl, beat them lightly with a fork to mix yolks and whites, then stir into the ricotta and season with black pepper.

Butter a 20cm soufflé or baking dish, then add the ricotta mixture and top with the reserved asparagus spears and Parmesan. Bake for thirty-five minutes till risen, its surface tinged with gold.

• More pudding than soufflé, but nevertheless light and airy. A tomato salad would work neatly here, dressed with basil and a dash of red wine vinegar.

BEETROOT, CARROTS, SUGAR SNAPS

Spring roots roasted. A creamy dressing.

Serves 2

young turnips 400g	yoghurt 3 heaped tablespoons
small carrots 200g	mayonnaise 3 heaped tablespoons
young beetroots 200g	parsley, chopped 2 tablespoons
olive oil 2 tablespoons	tarragon leaves, chopped
garlic 4 cloves	1 tablespoon
thyme 6 sprigs	sugar snap peas 150g

Set the oven at 200°C/Gas 6. Trim the turnips and cut them in half. Scrub the carrots and cut them in half lengthways. Scrub, but do not peel or slice, the beetroots. Place the vegetables in a roasting tin with the olive oil and peeled cloves of garlic, then add the sprigs of thyme. Season lightly, toss everything together, then roast for about thirty minutes until golden and tender.

Combine the yoghurt and mayonnaise with the parsley and tarragon. Season and set aside. Shred the sugar snap peas and fold into the other vegetables in the tin. Place everything on plates and spoon over the herb dressing.

• The only turnips worth roasting are the sweet, early-summer variety, no bigger than a golf ball. The older ones are better for casseroles and braising. Roasted, they can become a little bitter.
• Cutting the turnips in half before roasting gives the edges a chance to toast appetisingly. Shake the tin every now and again so that the vegetables brown evenly.
• Use young parsnips if you wish, or new potatoes instead of (or as well as) the turnips. For a summer version allow the vegetables to cool completely, then toss them in the dressing for serving with a grain salad.

GREEN FALAFEL, WATERMELON, YOGHURT

Creamy green chickpea cakes. A vibrant, piquant salsa.

Serves 4

chickpeas 2 × 400g cans	*For the salsa:*
broad beans 500g (weighed	cherry tomatoes 30
in pod)	a red onion
frozen peas 150g	watermelon 400g (skinned weight)
tarragon leaves 10g	small cornichons 20
parsley leaves 15g	
mint leaves, large 15	*To serve:*
spring onions 3, trimmed	a clove of garlic
	natural yoghurt 200g

Bring a large pan of water to the boil. Drain and rinse the chickpeas. Pod the beans and put them into the boiling water, cook for six to eight minutes, then remove from the water with a slotted spoon. Add the peas to the water, boil for three minutes, then drain.

Put the chickpeas, beans, peas, herb leaves and spring onions into a blender or food processor and reduce to a smooth green paste. Shape into twelve rounds the size of a golf ball, lightly flatten their tops, place them on a baking tray and chill for thirty minutes.

Set the oven at 200°C/Gas 6. Bake the falafel for thirty minutes or until lightly puffed up and dry to the touch.

For the salsa: quarter the tomatoes. Peel and finely dice the onion and mix with the tomatoes. Cut the watermelon into 3cm-thick triangles and add to the tomatoes. Halve the cornichons lengthways then add them to the salsa with a little of their liquid. Cover and refrigerate. Crush the garlic into the yoghurt, stir and add a little black pepper.

Serve the warm falafel with the chilled salad and the yoghurt and garlic.

KALE, BLUE CHEESE, ORECCHIETTE

Sustaining. Soothing. The goodness of kale.

Serves 3–4

kale 150g
milk 500ml
black peppercorns 10
bay leaves 3
garlic 3 cloves

orecchiette 200g
Parmesan 100g, grated
Shropshire Blue or other
    blue cheese 125g

Set the oven at 200°C/Gas 6. Bring a large pot of water to the boil. Discard the toughest of the kale stalks, then put the leaves into the pan. Leave them for a minute, until the colour brightens, then remove, cool under running water and squeeze dry. Reserve the cooking water.

Bring the milk to the boil with the peppercorns and bay leaves. As it reaches the boil, squash the garlic cloves flat and add them, then remove the pan from the heat and cover with a lid.

Boil the orecchiette in the kale water, generously salted, until toothsome, then drain. Put the kale, garlic and 90g of the Parmesan into a blender with 100ml of the milk and process till smooth. Transfer to a pan, put over a moderate heat and stir till hot, mixing in the remaining milk as you go (remove the peppercorns and bay).

Fold the drained pasta into the kale sauce, check the seasoning, adding pepper if you wish, then tip into a baking dish. Tuck crumbled pieces of the blue cheese into the pasta and sprinkle with the remaining Parmesan. Bake for 20–25 minutes till deep, golden brown.

• To cut down on the number of pans used, cook the kale and orecchiette in the same pan and heat the kale sauce in a deep baking dish that will go in the oven.

LENTILS, PEPPERS, GORGONZOLA

Sweet-sharp onion. Earthy lentils. Smoky roasted peppers.

Serves 3–4

a red onion, medium-sized
white wine vinegar 3 tablespoons
Romano peppers 6
olive oil 2 tablespoons
small, dark green lentils, such as
   Puy 150g
parsley 20g
Gorgonzola 200g

For the dressing:
basil 25g
parsley leaves 15g
a red chilli, small and mild,
   halved and deseeded
walnuts 50g
olive oil 6 tablespoons
lemon juice 3 tablespoons

Heat the oven to 200°C/Gas 6. Peel and finely slice the onion, put it in a small mixing bowl, then cover with the vinegar and set aside for at least forty minutes. Turn the onion over in the vinegar from time to time to ensure it marinates evenly.

Place the whole peppers in a roasting tin, add the olive oil and two tablespoons of water and bake for thirty to forty minutes until the peppers have collapsed and the skin is black in patches. Remove them from the oven.

Boil the lentils in a pan of deep, lightly salted water for twenty to twenty-five minutes till tender but with a little bite in them. Drain them in a sieve, put them in a bowl then add the drained onion.

When the peppers are ready, peel off their skins and discard, reserving their roasting juices. Tear the peppers into long, wide strips and put on a serving plate. Add the peppers' juices to the lentils.

Roughly chop 20g of parsley. If the leaves are small, I like to leave them whole. Stir into the lentils. Break the Gorgonzola into bite-sized pieces and add to the lentils. *(continued)*

Make the herb dressing: put the basil and the parsley leaves into a food processor or blender, together with the chilli, walnuts, olive oil and a pinch of sea salt and process to a coarse green paste. Taste the paste for seasoning and add salt and lemon juice as necessary.

Spoon the lentils and cheese on to the peppers, trickling over any dressing from the bottom of the bowl. Place a spoonful of the herb dressing on top.

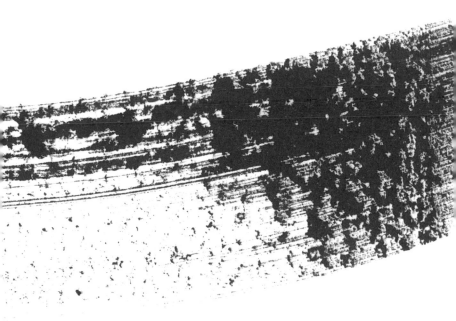

In the oven   143

ORZO, PEPPERS

Sweet peppers and soft pasta.

Serves 2

Romano peppers 6	orzo 250g
large spring onions 4	vegetable stock 600ml
garlic 6 cloves, peeled	
thyme 6 sprigs	*To finish:*
olive oil 6 tablespoons	young thyme leaves 1 teaspoon

Set the oven at 200°C/Gas 6. Place the peppers in a roasting tin. Cut the spring onions in half lengthways and tuck them amongst the peppers, together with the garlic cloves and thyme sprigs. Trickle over the olive oil and toss everything together.

Bake for thirty minutes, then tip in the orzo and stock and continue cooking for twenty minutes or until the pasta is al dente. Remove from the oven and fold in the extra thyme leaves. Check the seasoning and spoon onto plates.

• If the stock has not been absorbed by the pasta, place the tin over a moderate heat for a few minutes and let it reduce.

PEPPERS, PESTO, FETA

Robust flavours for high summer.

Serves 2

ripe peppers 2	olives 8
cherry tomatoes 6	basil pesto 8 teaspoons
feta 100g	olive oil

Set the oven at 180°C/Gas 4. Halve the peppers and remove and discard any stalks, cores or seeds. Put the peppers, cut side up, in a roasting tin.

Chop the cherry tomatoes and put them in a mixing bowl. Crumble the feta into large pieces and add to the tomatoes. Stone the olives, adding them to the bowl with a grinding of black pepper (no salt). Stir in the pesto, then spoon into the halved peppers. Pour enough olive oil into each to come up to the top. Bake for about twenty-five minutes, until the top is lightly brown.

• This is one of those dishes that seems more appropriate warm than hot, so leave the peppers to settle for twenty minutes before eating. While they are in the oven, you may want to cover the dish with kitchen foil to stop the pesto darkening.

• Fist-sized beefsteak tomatoes are a good vehicle for filling. Hollow out the cores and seeds and stuff with the feta, pesto, olives and small, golden tomatoes. A splash of red wine vinegar is a good trick, sprinkled over the dish just before it goes in the oven, to sharpen its edges.

ROAST NEW POTATOES, SPINACH SAUCE

Crisp and fudgy potatoes. Soothing green sauce.

Serves 2

new potatoes 500g
olive oil 5 tablespoons
young spinach leaves 100g
flaked almonds 4 tablespoons
butter 30g

garlic 2 cloves, sliced
grated Parmesan 3 tablespoons
double cream 250ml
pea shoots a handful

Set the oven at 200°C/Gas 6. Wash the potatoes. Put each one on a chopping board and make cuts, about the thickness of a pound coin, along the top, slicing almost through to the chopping board. The effect – hasselback – allows the potatoes to open as they roast, whilst at the same time they hold together.

Toss the potatoes in the oil and roast for about forty-five minutes till lightly crisp and nut brown. Meanwhile, wash the spinach. Put the still-wet leaves into a saucepan over a moderate heat, cover tightly with a lid and cook for a minute or two until the leaves start to wilt. Remove and refresh under cold running water.

Toast the almonds in a dry pan till golden. Remove the nuts, then add the butter and the garlic to the pan and fry till crisp. Squeeze the spinach leaves dry, then roughly chop and put in a pan with the grated Parmesan, double cream and a little pepper and salt. Warm gently.

Serve the potatoes with the spinach sauce, scattered with the almonds, garlic and pea shoots.

ROASTED PEPPER, TOMATO, FOCACCIA

The warmth of roast garlic. The sweetness of roast peppers.

Serves 2

focaccia 375g
Romano peppers 8
cherry or other small
    tomatoes 20
a head of garlic
olive oil 8 tablespoons
green beans 250g

basil leaves 8

For the dressing:
olive oil 6 tablespoons
an egg yolk
sherry vinegar 2 tablespoons

Preheat the oven to 200°C/Gas 6. Slice the focaccia horizontally, then put the pieces in a single layer in a roasting tin or baking tray. Place the peppers, tomatoes and the whole head of garlic on top of the focaccia. Trickle over the olive oil and roast for thirty minutes. The bread will soak up the juices and crisp lightly.

Peel the cooked garlic. Put three of the biggest cloves in a mortar with a pinch of salt, then crush to a paste. Stir in the 6 tablespoons of olive oil and set aside for twenty minutes. Trim the beans, cook for a minute or two in deep boiling water, then refresh in a bowl of iced water.

In a clean bowl, whisk the egg yolk, adding the garlic oil mixture a little at a time till you have a thickish dressing, then stir in the sherry vinegar and check the seasoning.

Tear the bread into pieces. Toss the beans, peppers, reserved garlic cloves, tomatoes and basil in the dressing and pile onto a large serving dish.

ROAST SPRING VEGETABLES, PEANUT SAUCE

Crunchy young vegetables. A rich, nutty sauce.

Serves 2

spring carrots 400g
young beetroots 500g
asparagus 400g
olive oil 4 tablespoons
thyme leaves 2 teaspoons, chopped
roasted, salted peanuts 100g

a medium, mild red chilli
peanut butter, crunchy 3 heaped tablespoons
juice of a lime
maple syrup 1 tablespoon
dark soy sauce 1 teaspoon

Set the oven at 200°C/Gas 6. Trim the spring carrots and slice them in half lengthways. Do the same with the young beetroots. Trim the asparagus, discarding any tough stalks. Put the vegetables in a mixing bowl and add the olive oil and thyme. Season with salt and black pepper and toss gently to coat everything. Tip into a roasting tin and roast in the preheated oven for twenty-five minutes until tender.

Toast the peanuts in a frying pan till they are deep gold and fragrant – a matter of a minute or two, no more. Transfer to a bowl. Finely chop the chilli and put it in a frying pan together with the peanut butter, followed by 60ml of water, the lime juice, maple syrup and soy. The sauce should be a rich chocolate brown and mildly spicy.

Remove the roast vegetables from the oven, scatter with the peanuts and serve with the sauce.

• You can use the sauce as a dip but I like to tip it out over the vegetables and toss everything together.

BROAD BEANS, SPRING GREENS, LASAGNE

Luscious, softly sustaining. A dinner for friends.

Serves 6

a small onion
cloves 3
milk 600ml
bay leaves 2
parsley sprigs 10g
leeks 700g
butter 40g
plain flour 3 heaped tablespoons
broad beans 400g (130g podded
    weight)
chard 150g

cabbage or spring greens 150g
button or small chestnut
    mushrooms 250g
olive oil 8 tablespoons, plus a
    little extra
tarragon, chopped 2 tablespoons
parsley, chopped 4 tablespoons
ricotta 300g
Parmesan 30g, grated
breadcrumbs 3 tablespoons

You will need a deep baking dish approximately 22 × 24cm.

Peel the onion, halve it and stud it with the cloves. Pour the milk into a saucepan, add the onion, bay leaves and parsley stalks, then bring almost to the boil. Remove from the heat and set aside to infuse. Set the oven at 200°C/Gas 6.

Trim the leeks, discarding any tough, dark green leaves, then thinly slice the rest and wash thoroughly. Melt the butter in a deep pan, add the leeks, then cover with a piece of greaseproof paper, pushing it down onto the leeks, and a lid. Let them cook for 8–10 minutes until they start to soften, then remove the paper, sprinkle over the flour and cook for a minute or two before pouring in the warm milk, removing the onion, bay and parsley as you go. Stir well and leave to simmer gently on a low to moderate heat.

Bring a large pot of water to the boil. Pod the broad beans and finely chop the chard stalks. Separate the leaves of the cabbage or spring greens
(continued)

and put into the boiling water. Soften for one minute, then remove and drain on kitchen paper. Repeat with the chard leaves. Finally, cook the broad beans for 5–6 minutes till just tender, then drain.

Thickly slice the mushrooms. Warm five tablespoons of the oil in a shallow pan, add the mushrooms and cook for five minutes or so till soft and golden. Stir the mushrooms, broad beans, tarragon and parsley into the leek sauce and season generously with salt and pepper.

Trickle a little oil in the bottom of the dish. Add two or three of the cabbage and chard leaves, then spoon in a third of the sauce. Cover with three more leaves, then some of the ricotta, followed by more sauce, ricotta and leaves until you have used them all, finishing with a layer of leaves. Mix together the chard stalks, Parmesan and breadcrumbs, then scatter over the surface and trickle over the remaining olive oil.

Bake for twenty-five minutes till the surface is crisp and golden.

• At first glance, daunting. Yet much of it involves little more than the chopping and blanching of vegetables. There is a white sauce to make, a couple of cheeses to grate and slice and the rest is an assembly job, layering vegetables, sauce and cheese in a dish. It's a full hour's work. The result is a creamy, herb-flecked main course that will generously feed six.

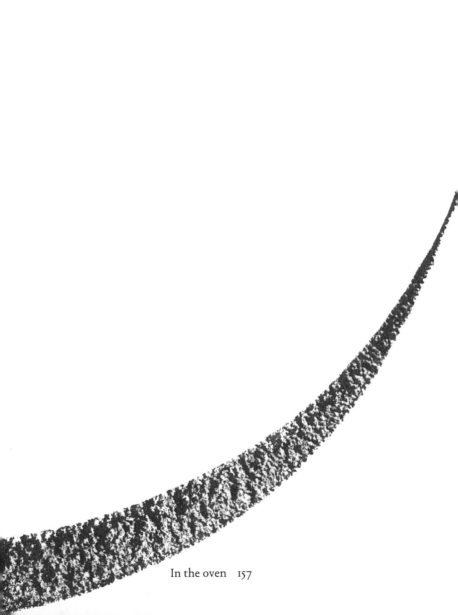

In the oven   157

TOMATOES, BASIL, BREADCRUMBS

Sweet summery juices. Crisp green crumbs.

Serves 4

basil 40g

fresh white bread 75g

olive oil 6 tablespoons,
  plus a little extra

assorted tomatoes 750g

Put the basil in a food processor with the bread and blend until you have green crumbs. Pour in the olive oil and briefly mix. Set the oven at 200°C/Gas 4.

Slice the tomatoes thickly, three or four good thick slices from each one, depending on their size. Layer them in a baking dish, seasoning each layer with a little salt, black pepper and the merest trickle of olive oil. Bake for thirty minutes.

Pile the basil crumbs on top of the tomatoes, press down gently and bake for another twenty-five minutes. Leave to rest for fifteen minutes before serving, spooning over the juices from the dish as you go.

TOMATOES, COUSCOUS, HARISSA

Luscious vegetables. The deep warmth of harissa.

Serves 2

assorted tomatoes 650g	golden raisins 75g
garlic 1 clove, crushed	mint 15g
olive oil	parsley 15g
a red onion	harissa paste 1 tablespoon
vegetable stock 400ml	sesame seeds 2 tablespoons
couscous 100g	

Set the oven at 200°C/Gas 6. Put the tomatoes (red, orange, yellow, green, cherry, etc.) into a roasting tin with the garlic and a little oil. Peel and slice the onion and add it to the tomatoes with a seasoning of salt and black pepper. Roast for about twenty-five to thirty minutes until the tomatoes are soft and the skins lightly browned.

Bring the vegetable stock to the boil. Place the couscous in a heatproof bowl, then pour the boiling stock over, fold in the raisins, cover and leave for fifteen minutes. Roughly chop the mint and parsley leaves, discarding the stalks.

Use a fork to lightly crush the tomatoes so the juices bleed into the pan, then stir in the harissa paste. Toast the sesame seeds for a minute or two in a dry pan till golden. Stir most of the chopped herbs through the couscous with a fork. Serve the roast tomatoes and their juices on top of the couscous, and sprinkle the reserved herbs and sesame seeds on top.

• It is perfectly fine to use water to plump up your couscous, but I like using stock, in this case vegetable, to add flavour to the bland grain. Pour over enough boiling water to cover the couscous by a good 3–4cm. Covering the bowl with a plate or lid will help it stay hot during the ten

(continued)

minutes or so it takes for the grains to sponge up the liquid. No further heating required.

• If time is tight, you could grill the tomatoes and onions, setting the roasting tin a good way from the heat, and turning the vegetables from time to time as they cook.

• This also makes a cracking summer salad. Cook as above, but let the couscous and the tomatoes cool a little before serving. Instead of finishing with mint and parsley, make a herb mixture of chopped basil and finely grated lemon zest, then toss with toasted, finely crumbed ciabatta and a glug of olive oil.

ON A PLATE

The most beautiful thing I have ever seen on a plate was a mushroom. To be accurate, a single slice of mushroom. A piece of puffball the size of a schnitzel. Cooked by Margot Henderson when she was at the French House in Soho many years ago, I have never forgotten the quiet majesty of that vast slice of fungi, the colour of old parchment, unsullied by sauce or garnish. There may have been half a lemon with it.

I am rarely happier than when putting a plate of food in front of someone. That said, I don't think it should be crowded. I have a loathing of piles of food, what I call the dog's dinner approach. Yes, there should be enough, feeding people is all about generosity, but I prefer to put food on a dish in the centre of the table, pass round some plates and let everyone help themselves.

I think of 'plate food' more as assemblies, those collections we put together from the fridge – a few pieces of grilled aubergine or courgette; slices of tomato dressed with basil and red wine vinegar; a soft mound of red pepper hummus. On other days there may be a tangle of wide pappardelle or a round of thick toast spread with a mash of bright green peas. A mound of mozzarella maybe, with fried greens and sizzled chilli or slices of tomato and crumbled salty ricotta. Note that this is all stuff that comes with a dressing rather than a sauce. Sauces need a bowl and spoon in my book. Better still, a wedge of bread.

A plate gives us the chance to make the food look good, rather than the constituent parts sitting on top of each other as they do in a bowl. The food can breathe. I don't feel dinner should ever be plated in the contrived, precious style of a fine-dining restaurant, but it can be given the sort of care and thought that can't always happen when you ladle something into a bowl. On a wide, flat plate, you can take a moment to create food that looks attractive, and yet has an entirely organic, almost accidental feel to it. My own rule is never to 'arrange' food on a plate. It looks agonised and contorted and ultimately a bit unwelcoming. It lacks heart and soul.

My natural instinct is always to put food on a capacious platter or large, shallow dish and put it on the table together with a large spoon and fork – an invitation to tuck in. Such a way of serving allows everyone to take as much, or as little, as they wish. Plating food for people always smacks a bit of portion control. Something that should play no part in eating with friends and family. Worse still, the cook's over-generosity can be over-facing for some of us, like myself, with an innate curiosity and desire (for which read greed) to taste everything, but in small quantities.

A lightly dressed salad will look tempting on a plate, where the dressing can collect in the folds and crevices. As does a slice of tart or pie. A little dish of vegetables or grains or pasta on the side is a delightful accompaniment to anything. But piled on the same plate it can look a mess. A simple, unfussy style is useful when you want to put a fridge-raid together without making it into a salad. So an oozy hillock of Gorgonzola will complement a few curls of pink pickled onion, and some warm lentils you have tossed with olive oil; a tangle of cold, spicy noodles from last night, some sharp, salty pickles and a stray, but nevertheless welcome slice of halloumi.

BEETROOT, CURRY LEAVES, CRISP ONIONS

Sweet spice. Mild spice.

Serves 2

For the rice:

white basmati rice 120g	onions, medium 2
bay leaves 3	olive oil 2 tablespoons
green cardamom pods 6	garlic 2 cloves
black peppercorns 6	coriander seeds 1 teaspoon
a cinnamon stick	curry leaves 20
cloves 2 or 3	cooked beetroot 4 small
cumin seeds a pinch	yoghurt 100g

Wash the rice three times in a bowl of warm water, then put it in a small saucepan with the bay leaves, the cardamom pods, lightly crushed, peppercorns, cinnamon stick, cloves and cumin seeds. Pour in enough water to cover and leave 2cm of water above the rice.

Bring the water to the boil, season with salt, then turn down the heat so the water simmers and cover tightly with a lid. Cook for ten minutes, then remove from the heat but leave covered with the lid.

While the rice cooks, peel and roughly chop the onions, then cook in the olive oil in a shallow pan till pale gold and translucent. Peel and finely slice the garlic and add to the onions, along with the coriander seeds, and continue cooking till the garlic is soft. Stir in the curry leaves. Cut the cooked beetroot into quarters and let it warm through with the onions, which should now be turning golden.

Lift the lid from the rice, stir with a fork to separate the grains, then divide between two plates or shallow dishes. Spoon the beetroot, onions and curry leaves over the rice and serve with the yoghurt.

BROAD BEANS, PEA SHOOTS, SALTED RICOTTA

Clean summer flavours. Salty and bright.

Serves 2

broad beans 500g (weighed in pod)	pea shoots 25g
	olive oil
small tomatoes 150g	salted ricotta, grated
parsley a small bunch	4 tablespoons

Bring a saucepan of water to the boil, salt it lightly then add the beans and let them cook for four or five minutes. Drain the beans and plunge them into iced water. Pop the largest from their skins, but leave the smaller beans be.

Slice each tomato into four and put them in a bowl. Remove the leaves from the parsley and chop enough for two heaped tablespoons. Add the parsley to the tomatoes together with the broad beans and pea shoots.

Dress with a little olive oil, gently turning the ingredients over till finely coated. Divide between plates, then scatter over the salted ricotta and serve.

• Soaking the pea shoots in a bowl of ice and water for twenty minutes will put a spring in their step.

• A salad as simple as this relies on the quality of the ingredients alone. The beans should be young and sweet; the tomatoes, I think, should be bright-flavoured and crisp rather than ripe and soft. Those green-shouldered early summer fruits are probably ideal.

• If salted ricotta proves evasive, I suggest feta. It has the salty tang the salad needs.

BURRATA, BROCCOLI, LENTILS

Milky, fragile cheese. Earthy lentils. Sizzling, chilli-hot greens.

Serves 2

small green or brown lentils 80g
olive oil
broccoli a medium-sized head
garlic 2 cloves
butter 30g
a red chilli, medium
burrata 2 balls

Cook the lentils in deep, lightly salted boiling water for about twenty minutes till tender but toothsome. Drain them, toss in a splash of olive oil and set aside.

Slice the green florets from the top of the broccoli. Shave any tough bits from the stalks with a vegetable peeler, then cut the largest into small pieces. Leave any small ones whole.

Bring a pan of water to the boil and add the broccoli stalks. Let them cook for a couple of minutes, then remove, drain and set aside. Peel and finely slice the garlic cloves, then fry in the butter in a shallow pan till deep gold, crisp and fragrant. Remove them from the pan and drain on kitchen paper.

Finely chop and fry the chilli in the garlic pan, adding a little more butter or oil if necessary, then, as soon as it is soft, add the broccoli florets. Cook for a couple of minutes till tender, then add the cooked stalks and continue cooking for a further two minutes till hot.

Drain the cheese, put one burrata on each plate, then spoon over the sizzling broccoli and lentils. Scatter the crisp garlic over the top and serve.

• The warm, crisp garlic and hot chilli-spiked greens are simply gorgeous with the cool milky burrata. It is worth taking care with frying the garlic, letting it sizzle quietly over a gentle heat, so it browns lightly and evenly as it crisps. Anything more than walnut brown and it will be bitter.

FENNEL, RADISH, YOGHURT

A cooling salad for the hottest of days.

Serves 2, with other dishes

natural yoghurt 100g
soured cream 100g
olive oil 1 tablespoon
mint leaves 12

fennel 240g
a watermelon radish or
    small mooli
burrata 1

Mix together the natural yoghurt, soured cream, olive oil, a grinding of sea salt and another of black pepper. Shred the mint leaves into the dressing.

Finely slice the fennel and the watermelon radish, then toss them in the dressing. Leave the salad for twenty minutes before serving with the burrata.

MUSHROOMS, PEAS, TOAST

Bosky fungi. The verdant green of peas.

Serves 2

frozen peas 200g	portobello mushroom 1 large
rocket 50g	king oyster mushrooms 2
juice of half a lemon	butter 40g
tarragon 10g	garlic 1 clove
olive oil	bread 2 thick slices

Cook the peas in boiling water for three or four minutes till tender. Drain and tip them into the bowl of a food processor with the rocket, the lemon juice and the leaves from the tarragon. Blend in 80ml of olive oil to give a smooth, bright green purée, then set aside.

Wipe the mushrooms and slice them into pieces about 1cm thick. In a large, shallow pan, warm a couple of tablespoons of olive oil with the butter over a moderate heat. As it starts to sizzle, add the garlic, thinly sliced, then the mushrooms. Let the mushrooms soften. Season with salt and black pepper.

Toast the bread, then spread generously with some of the pea purée. Divide the hot mushrooms between the toasts and serve.

• You could use two distinct types of mushroom here – the firm, cheap varieties, such as chestnut or portobello, and then something more tender, such as shimeji or enoki. The former need frying to a deep nutty brown before you add the more tender varieties. The latter are fragile and should be stirred in only when the firm mushrooms are almost cooked, to preserve their delicate texture.

NOODLES, SPROUTED BEANS, PEANUTS

Light, clean, uplifting. A salad with a spark.

Serves 4

sprouted mung beans 100g
a medium-sized carrot
brown rice noodles 100g
a medium-sized cucumber
coriander a large handful
mint leaves 15
pak choi 2 crisp, juicy heads
roasted, salted peanuts 40g

For the dressing:

juice of 2 limes
light soy sauce 2 teaspoons
palm sugar 2 teaspoons
a small hot red or green chilli
garlic 2 small new-season cloves

Rinse the mung beans under icy-cold running water and drain. Scrub the carrot, slice thinly lengthways, then slice again into matchstick-size strips. Pour boiling water over the noodles in a heatproof bowl and leave to soak for 10 minutes till swollen and tender. (Check the cooking instructions on the packet depending on the noodles you are using.)

Lightly peel the cucumber, slice in half from stalk to tip, then scrape out the seeds and core with a teaspoon and discard them. Cut the cucumber into pencil-thick slices. Remove the leaves from the coriander, leave any small ones whole, and roughly chop the larger ones. Do the same with the mint leaves. Shred the pak choi.

Toss the mung beans, carrot, cucumber, herbs and pak choi together. Drain the noodles and toss with the vegetables and herbs.

Make the dressing: mix together the juice of the limes, the light soy and sugar. Finely chop the red chilli and add to the dressing. Peel, smash, then finely chop the garlic, then add to the dressing and toss with the noodle mixture. Finally, coarsely chop the peanuts and scatter over the salad.

(continued)

• Use whatever noodles you have around for this crisp, light salad. I have suggested brown rice noodles but only because that is what I had in the house. The dressing is at its most refreshing when sharp, sweet and hot, but tweak it to your liking, adding more palm sugar or lime juice as you wish.

POTATOES, SPINACH, POMEGRANATE

Mild, earthy spices. A creamy dressing. The sourness of pomegranates.

Serves 2

new potatoes 300g
groundnut oil 2 tablespoons
curry powder a teaspoon or 2
mayonnaise 3 tablespoons

soured cream 4 tablespoons
young spinach leaves 50g
spring onions 3
half a pomegranate

Cook the potatoes in deep, salted boiling water till tender. A matter of twenty minutes or so depending on their size.

In a small mixing bowl, mix the oil, curry powder and mayonnaise, then stir in the soured cream.

Drain the potatoes, then fold them into the dressing with the spinach leaves. Finely shred the spring onions, add to the salad and pile onto plates. Break the pomegranate into individual seeds and scatter them over.

TOMATO, PEAS, FETA

The salty tang of feta, the vibrant crunch of raw peas.

Serves 2

half a lemon
olive oil 6 tablespoons
mint leaves 8
parsley leaves a handful

tomatoes 3 medium-sized
peas 500g (weight with pods)
feta 100g
radishes 10

Squeeze the juice from the lemon into a blender, then pour in the olive oil. Add the mint and parsley, season with a little salt and process to a thick, bright green dressing.

Slice the tomatoes, lay them in a single layer on two serving plates, then moisten them with a spoonful of the dressing. Grind over a little black pepper, then cover and set aside for a good twenty minutes.

Pod the peas. You should be left with about 175g of peas. Chop them roughly, then scoop them into a small bowl. Crumble the feta into tiny pieces and fold through the peas followed by the dressing.

Trim the radishes, put them on top of the tomatoes, then divide the pea mixture between the two plates.

• This is the sort of thing to put together at the last moment, and much depends on the freshness of the tomatoes, raw peas and the sprightly dressing.
• Add young fennel, courgettes or green beans to the salad as the season progresses.

TOMATO, BEANS, BREAD

High summer.

Serves 4–6
green 'French' beans 200g
light, open-textured bread 200g
olive oil
assorted tomatoes 850g
spring onions 3
black olives, pitted 16

For the dressing:
red wine vinegar 2 tablespoons
olive oil 6 tablespoons
new garlic 1 clove
basil 15 leaves

Put a pan of water on to boil. Top and tail the beans, then cook them in the boiling water for three or four minutes till tender, remove from the heat and plunge into iced water.

Warm your oven grill. Tear the bread into large, jagged pieces, roughly 4cm in diameter, and spread them out in a single layer on a baking sheet. Trickle about four tablespoons of olive oil over the bread, then grill till golden brown.

Make the dressing: pour the vinegar into a small bowl, then beat in the olive oil and a little salt and pepper. Peel and very finely slice the garlic and add to the dressing. Stir half the basil into the dressing and set aside for a few minutes.

Slice the tomatoes and put them into a large salad bowl. Finely slice the spring onions and add to the tomatoes. Dip the toasted bread into the dressing and add to the bowl. Drain the green beans and pat dry, then add to the salad with the olives and reserved basil. Pour over the dressing and toss gently together with the tomatoes and bread.

• As much as I like the luscious bread and tomato salads of high summer, I always feel they need a little contrast, something crisp to balance the

(continued)

softness of the saturated bread. To this end I have introduced, at the last minute, crisp hearts of iceberg lettuce, raw courgette (a mistake) and lightly cooked broad beans that somehow felt out of place. Green beans, crisp, bright and pencil-thin, hit the spot, offering a much-needed change of texture.

ON THE GRILL

I would be lost without my cast-iron griddle, with its well-worn, blackened furrows. You heat it up, slap on a few slices of aubergine, press them down onto the heat with a palette knife or a weight, then lift them off and dress with olive oil, lemon juice and crushed basil leaves. At their side goes a jagged slice of feta or a piece of rosemary-scented goat's cheese. A slice of toast rubbed with garlic and crushed tomatoes and you have lunch.

The deep smoky notes, the delicious battle-scars and the crisp edges all add to the appeal of cooking on the griddle. If I could only have one method with which to cook my food, it would be this. But an 'oven' grill is useful too. It allows a large amount of food to be cooked at one time, and the involvement of more oil and herbs, both of which char all too quickly on a griddle pan. The flavours are less smoky and archaic, but control is often easier, and you can see what is happening without lifting the food from the heat.

In deepest summer, grilled food seems more appropriate than at any other time. The flavour of outdoor cooking. This being a book of ideas for simple, everyday eating excludes me from going into detail about lighting the charcoal grill, but all the recipes in this chapter, and a few elsewhere in the book, could be adapted easily for those who wish to get the charcoal out. The smoke will add another level of seasoning.

I now cook things on the griddle or under the grill that I wouldn't have done years ago. Asparagus (just add a spoon of miso-infused mayo), aubergines (toss with feta cheese, yoghurt and mint) and slices of king oyster mushrooms. The bars of the grill also do much for lumps of polenta and slices of halloumi, shavings of courgette and summer squash and, most recently, halved little gem lettuces and wedges of spring cabbage. The latter needs a dressing of some sort, and I usually go for a lemony olive oil one, or better still, lowering the blackened leaves into a bowl of soup.

Many summer vegetables will benefit from a few minutes on or under the grill, long-stemmed broccoli being a good example. But to save you the trouble, a few that don't work include beetroot, spring carrots and cucumber. Tomatoes work splendidly cooked under the oven grill, but not on the griddle, where they tend to lose their precious juices. I often cut large tomatoes (though not the watery beefsteak fruits) into thick slices, season with olive oil, salt and crumbled rosemary and cook under the heat till they scorch here and there. They are then lifted onto a platter, put on the table with a generous crumble of sheep's cheese and sprinkled with red wine vinegar and the occasional caper. Chunks of bread are passed round, dipped into the warm tomatoey, vinegary juices, then eaten with slices of the jelly-fleshed, blackened tomato.

AUBERGINE, FETA, YOGHURT

Smoky aubergine. Cool, minted yoghurt.

Serves 3 as a side dish, 2 as a main

small aubergines 250g	parsley leaves a large handful
olive oil 100ml	feta cheese 100g
natural yoghurt 150g	pickled onions or chillies 3
chopped mint leaves 2 tablespoons	whole, small mint leaves to finish

Get a griddle pan hot. Cut the aubergines lengthways into 1cm-thick slices, score them on one side, then place them on the griddle and let them cook, watching their progress carefully, until they are soft and nicely browned.

Pour the olive oil into a mixing bowl and season it with a little salt and black pepper. As each piece of aubergine comes from the grill, push it down into the olive oil, then set aside whilst you make the dressing.

Put the yoghurt in a medium-sized bowl and add the chopped mint. Roughly chop the parsley, leaving the smaller, younger leaves whole, then stir all into the yoghurt with a little ground black pepper. Crumble the feta cheese into small pieces and fold into the yoghurt.

Spoon the feta dressing onto a serving dish. Lay the aubergine slices, without their oil, on top. Slice the pickled onions or chillies, then add them to the dish. Scatter over the whole, small mint leaves, then spoon over a little of the aubergine olive oil marinade.

• On this occasion, I cook the aubergines without oiling them, then put them in the seasoned olive oil. They emerge, twenty minutes later, luscious and silkily soft. (And you have avoided filling your kitchen with smoke.)
• Grilled aubergines nestling in a thick dressing of minted yoghurt and feta cheese is something I put on the table as a main course with warm flatbread.

GRILLED LETTUCE, CARROT SOUP

Pure flavours for a summer's day.

Serves 2–4

carrots 1kg
vegetable stock 1 litre
bay leaves 3
black peppercorns 6

little gem lettuces 2
micro leaves and herbs such
    as coriander and sorrel

Roughly chop the carrots. Put them into a large saucepan with the stock, bay leaves and peppercorns and bring to the boil. Salt lightly, then lower the heat to a simmer and leave for twenty minutes until the carrots are soft.

Remove the bay leaves and blend the carrots and their cooking liquor to a smooth purée in a blender or food processor. Return to the saucepan and check the seasoning.

Get a griddle pan really hot. Slice the lettuces in half lengthways and place, cut side down, on the griddle. Press firmly down with a heavy weight and leave to cook for six to seven minutes until the cut side is golden brown and starting to crisp.

Spoon the hot soup into bowls, add the grilled lettuces and finish with the fresh herbs.

• A deep-flavoured vegetable stock is needed here, and some carrots with plenty of flavour. The bunches of thin, sweet, spring carrots have little to offer in terms of flavour, so I suggest using maincrop carrots here.

COURGETTES, RICOTTA, PINE KERNELS

The heady scent of deepest summer.

Serves 2

courgettes 400g
olive oil
pine kernels 2 tablespoons

basil leaves 10g
lemon juice 1 tablespoon
ricotta 250g

Using a vegetable peeler, cut the courgettes into long, wide ribbons, running the peeler down their length.

Put the courgettes into a wide mixing bowl with four tablespoons of oil and a grinding of sea salt and black pepper. Lightly toast the pine kernels in a dry, shallow pan till pale gold. Warm a ridged griddle pan, then add the courgettes and let them cook till they are golden and lightly blistered on both sides.

Pour a couple of tablespoons of olive oil into a bowl, then shred the basil leaves and add them. Tip in the toasted pine kernels, add the lemon juice and mix together.

As the courgettes come from the grill, tip them into the basil and lemon dressing and toss gently to coat.

Place a mound of fresh ricotta on each plate then add the grilled ribbons of courgette. Spoon the basil and pine kernel dressing over and serve. I think some bruschetta would be good here.

• Watch the pine kernels closely on their short route from ivory to golden brown. They burn in seconds and will be extremely bitter if they do. There is no need to salt the courgettes. Place the strips flat on the griddle, then, when the underside is patchily gold and black, turn them over with a pair of kitchen tongs and cook the other side. They are best dressed whilst still warm, as the gentle heat teases out the flavour of the basil.

(continued)

• Tarragon and mint, chopped or torn, will introduce notes of aniseed and coolness to the dish if you use them with, or instead of the basil. You could involve garlic if you like, either crushed into a paste and tossed with the raw courgettes, or roasted and mashed into the basil dressing. You could also bring in some ribbons of cooked pappardelle, folding them through the grilled courgettes and dressing.

HALLOUMI, MELON, CHILLI

Salty, squeaky cheese. Chilled fruit. Hot spice.

Serves 2

spring onions 2	olive oil
small tomatoes 6	ciabatta 4 slices
chilli, red 1 medium	halloumi 250g
watermelon 200g	coriander 2 sprigs
cantaloupe melon 200g	

Finely dice the spring onions. Roughly chop the tomatoes, then finely chop the red chilli. Cut the melons into large pieces, removing the skin as you go. Toss the spring onions, tomatoes, chilli, watermelon and cantaloupe with a couple of tablespoons of olive oil and place in the fridge to chill.

In a shallow pan, warm a generous film of olive oil and use it to fry the ciabatta slices. Brown them nicely on both sides. As the second side starts to turn gold, spoon over some of the olive oil from around it. Remove from the pan.

Cut the halloumi into two large slices, then let them cook, brushed with a little oil, on a ridged griddle pan, till golden brown. Divide the salsa between two plates, then place the bread and the halloumi on it.

• A dish of contrasts. I like to chill the watermelon thoroughly, to provide a cool contrast for the hot, chilli-spiced toast and sizzling halloumi. The hot elements of this salad should be just that, and the melon should be refreshingly cold. Take care not to over-brown the cheese, as it loses its point when overcooked. A few flashes of gold on the surface is all you need.
• Cantaloupe melon is good here, as would be slices of sweet, ripe mango. If the sweetness of melon isn't your thing, then take a selection of tomatoes, from small sweet-sour yellow cherry tomatoes to large, knobbly Marmande instead.

POLENTA, SPINACH, PARMESAN

Something substantial for a cool summer's day.

Serves 4

fine polenta 250g	*For the spinach sauce:*
parsley leaves 35g	spinach 300g
spring onions 3	double cream 500ml
oregano 8g	grated Parmesan 5 tablespoons

Put 750ml of water on to boil, then, when it is fiercely bubbling, salt it generously and rain in the polenta, stirring as it falls. If you do this from a height, it will lessen the chances of the polenta forming lumps. Lower the heat so the polenta bubbles lazily, and keep stirring regularly, getting right into the corners of the pan with your wooden spoon. Take great care not to let the polenta scald you – it sends up volcano-like eruptions as it cooks.

Continue cooking and stirring until the polenta is thick enough for the spoon to stand up in the pan. Roughly chop the parsley, spring onions and leaves from the oregano and stir into the hot polenta. Lightly oil a 24 × 35cm baking tray and scrape the polenta onto it, smoothing it with the wooden spoon to fill the tin. Leave to set.

Wash the spinach and pile, still wet, into a pan with a lid. Steam for a minute or two, occasionally turning the spinach with kitchen tongs. Remove from the pan and squeeze any remaining water out. Empty, rinse and dry the pan, return to the heat, pour in the cream, stir in the spinach, then add the grated Parmesan. Season with a little pepper and set aside.

Using a 6cm cookie cutter or glass as a template, cut discs from the polenta. Heat a griddle pan over a moderate to high flame, place the discs on the hot bars of the griddle and leave until lightly crisp, then carefully turn with a palette knife and cook the other side.

Spoon the spinach sauce onto plates, then put the polenta discs on top of the sauce.

ON THE HOB

Most of my spring and summer dinners are cooked on the hob. A plate of spaghetti dressed with crème fraîche, samphire and lemon; a bowl of green minestrone or perhaps new potatoes with wild garlic, or spinach and cream. Other regulars are a purée of cauliflower with toasted florets or a plate of chickpeas folded through steaming, roasted wheat.

A dish of pasta can often be on the table in minutes: wide ribbons of pappardelle with green peas and ricotta; fettucine with pesto and preserved artichokes; or what is possibly my favourite pasta dish of all, the almost absurdly simple trofie with melted Pecorino and parsley. There are sautéed suppers of potatoes and crushed sweet-sour tomatoes; stews of soft summer squash, spinach and chickpeas and couscous with beans and oranges. There are fried mushrooms for tossing with tagliatelle and bucatini with courgettes and grated cheese, asparagus with a poached egg or miso mayonnaise, a summer pilaf freckled with broad beans and herb butter.

The hob allows flexibility. Dinner can be sautéed, deep-fried or steamed. It can be simmered under a lid, or boiled in deep water as salty as the North Sea. The latter option can involve ribbons, curls and tubes of pasta, tossed in a sauce or dressing that can be made in the time it takes the pasta to cook: olive oil, lemon and crushed herbs; a cream sauce freshened with grated lemon zest and given warmth with preserved green peppercorns, or ricotta cheese with Parmesan and crushed raw green peas.

A high-sided pan gives you the chance to make a summer soup that can putter away quietly whilst you get on with other things. The high sides prevent it from boiling to nothing as it might in a wide, shallow pan. A mixture of broad beans, peas and courgettes perhaps, or simply a vegetable stock into which you stir white miso paste and steamed spring greens. A handful of noodles – so useful for adding heft to light spring and summer meals – is unlikely to go amiss.

ARTICHOKE, TAGLIATELLE

Fragrant, subtle, understated.

Serves 2

garlic 3 cloves
olive oil 100ml
tagliatelle 180g

marinated artichokes 500g
basil 30g

Peel and finely chop the garlic. Warm the olive oil in a shallow pan, scatter in the garlic and leave to cook for a minute or two over a moderate heat, until a pale, nut brown.

Bring a large, deep pan of water to the boil, salt generously, add the pasta and let it cook, at a rolling boil, until tender but firm, then drain in a colander.

Reserve two halves of artichoke per person, then blend together the garlic, warm olive oil, remaining artichokes and basil using a food processor or blender. Check the seasoning, then toss the dressing with the drained pasta and the reserved artichokes.

• The artichokes I like for this are those that have been halved and marinated in oil and herbs. They can be bought loose at the deli counter or in jars.
• A squeeze of lemon juice, or perhaps a grating of Parmesan, might be in order here. Or spoonfuls of pure white ricotta.

ASPARAGUS, MISO, MUSTARD

Green spears. A savoury dip.

Serves 2

asparagus 250g

an egg yolk

groundnut oil 80ml

white miso paste 2 tablespoons

grain mustard 2 teaspoons

a small lemon

chives 6

Trim the asparagus, discarding any tough ends. Bring a shallow pan of water to the boil, lower in the asparagus and cook until done to your liking. The exact time will depend on the thickness of your spears. Start checking after seven minutes.

Put the egg yolk into a mixing bowl together with a small pinch of salt. Pour in the oil, slowly, beating continually with a balloon whisk, as if you were making mayonnaise. Beat in the white miso paste and the mustard, whisking until you have a thickish dressing. Finely grate most of the zest from the lemon, taking care not to include any of the bitter white pith underneath, and stir into the miso mayonnaise. Check the seasoning.

Finely chop the chives. Drain the asparagus, divide between two plates, then spoon over the miso dressing. Finish with the remaining zest and the chives.

• Use the mild white 'shiro' miso here, not the stronger, saltier, brown variety.

• This is something to put on the table with dishes such as steamed brown rice or quinoa and perhaps a bowl of instant miso soup.

EGGS, POTATOES

A humble but sustaining dish.

Serves 2

new potatoes 450g
tomato passata 350ml
bottled guindilla chillies 4

cherry tomatoes 200g
spring onions 3
eggs 2

Boil the potatoes in deep, lightly salted water for twenty minutes till tender. Drain and crush them lightly with a fork, breaking the skin and allowing the steam to escape. Tip them into a medium-sized, high-sided frying pan and pour over the passata. Tuck the chillies amongst the potatoes. Season generously.

Halve the tomatoes and chop the spring onions. Place the passata over a moderate heat, then as it warms, make two hollows with the back of a spoon in which to cook the eggs. Break the eggs into the hollows, letting the yolks and whites fall gently amongst the potatoes, and cover with a lid. Cook for two or three minutes until the egg whites have set and the yolks are still runny.

Remove from the heat and scatter over the onions and tomatoes.

BROAD BEANS, FLAGEOLETS, COURGETTES

Spring soup. A bean feast.

Serves 4

broad beans in the pod 400g
baby leeks 200g
spring onions 200g
olive oil
small courgettes 200g
flageolet beans 1 × 400g can

peas (fresh or frozen) 200g
  (podded weight)
vegetable stock 1 litre
chives 20g
parsley a handful
grated Parmesan, to serve

Pod the broad beans, boil them in lightly salted water, then drain and cool under cold running water. Unless they are really young and small, at this point I like to pop them out of their pale skins.

Thickly slice the leeks (I like to do them diagonally). Thinly slice the spring onions. Cook the leeks and onions in a saucepan, in a couple of tablespoons of olive oil, covered with a piece of greaseproof paper or baking parchment. This will encourage them to steam and soften rather than fry. You want them to be tender, but they shouldn't brown.

Cut the courgettes into short lengths. When the leeks and spring onions are soft and still bright green, remove the greaseproof paper, add the courgettes, the flageolet beans, drained and rinsed, the peas and then the stock. Bring to the boil, turn down to a simmer, then add the chives, chopped into short lengths. Roughly chop the parsley and stir into the soup. Season and pass round a dish of grated Parmesan.

BROAD BEANS, COUSCOUS, PINE KERNELS

Soft couscous. Crisp radishes. Toasted pine kernels. Gentle spring flavours.

Serves 2

couscous 80g
broad beans 200g (podded weight)
pine kernels 25g
oranges 2
mint leaves 10

parsley a small bunch
radishes 6
spring onions 3
olive oil

Put the kettle on to boil. Tip the couscous into a heatproof mixing bowl, then pour enough of the boiling water over to cover it by 2cm. Set aside for about fifteen minutes, covered by a plate, till the couscous has absorbed all the liquid.

Cook the broad beans in lightly salted boiling water for five or six minutes till just tender, then drain. Pop them out of their papery skins by pressing them between thumb and finger.

In a dry pan, toast the pine kernels till golden, shaking the pan from time to time to help them to brown easily. Remove the peel from the oranges with a knife, taking care to cut away all the bitter white pith under the skin, then cut each orange into about five thin slices.

Finely chop the mint and parsley leaves. (You will need a good couple of handfuls of chopped parsley.) Trim and finely slice the radishes and spring onions. Run a fork through the couscous to separate the grains, then add the chopped herbs, the broad beans and the pine kernels, then the radishes and spring onions. Season generously.

Serve the couscous, trickled with olive oil, with the slices of orange.

• For a quick midweek meal, I would use instant couscous. You can use boiling water to soak it, but I also like to use vegetable or chicken stock if

(continued)

I have some. Running a fork through the couscous is essential to separate and lighten the texture. It is better not to make the salad more than an hour in advance, after which time the texture may suffer.

• You need something crisp to contrast with the general softness of the couscous. Cucumber for instance, radishes, celery, lightly cooked green beans cut into small dice, grated carrot, toasted nuts, especially flaked almonds. I also like adding toasted seeds such as sunflower, sesame and pumpkin.

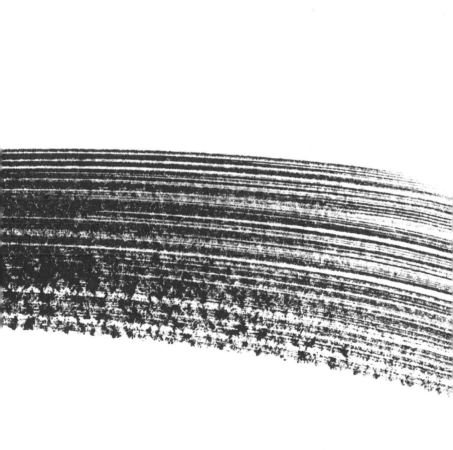

BROAD BEANS, NEW POTATOES, TOMATOES

A simple summer vegetable stew. A hint of early garlic.

Serves 3

broad beans in their pods 600g
new potatoes 350g
butter 20g
olive oil 2 tablespoons

garlic 2 cloves
cherry tomatoes 150g
pea shoots a handful, about 25g

Put a pan of water on to boil and salt it lightly. Pod the broad beans, then cook them in the boiling water for three to five minutes depending on their size. Remove from the heat, drain the beans and cool briefly under cold running water. Squeeze the larger beans from their papery skins. Leave the smaller ones intact.

Slice the new potatoes in half lengthways. Warm the butter and oil in a shallow pan, add the potatoes, cut side down at first, and let them cook for fifteen minutes or so, until lightly golden. Test them for tenderness, turning them once or twice as they fry so they colour evenly. Peel and finely slice the garlic, adding it to the pan halfway through cooking, so you just get the faintest hint rather than full-on flavour.

Cut the cherry tomatoes in half, then add them to the potatoes and let them cook for three or four minutes, crushing them gently as they cook with the back of a spoon to encourage their juices to flow into the pan. For the last minute of cooking, add the pea shoots, just enough time for their colour to darken and their texture to relax, then fold in the broad beans, check the seasoning and serve.

• Cooking the tomatoes briefly keeps their flavours light and fresh. Crushing them lightly with the back of spoon as they cook allows the juices to run, giving more of a dressing than a sauce.

BUCATINI, COURGETTES, SPINACH

Spring vegetables and skinny pasta. A light cream sauce.

Serves 2

spinach 200g	olive oil
sugar snap peas 125g	parsley a small bunch
bucatini 200g	double cream 125ml
large courgette 1	grated Parmesan, to serve
butter 30g	

Rinse the spinach, removing any tough stems. While the leaves are still wet, cook them for a minute or two in a pan with a tight lid, so they soften in their own steam. If you are worried about them sticking, add a tablespoon or two of water.

As soon as the spinach has wilted, plunge it into a bowl of iced water to stop it cooking, squeeze it dry with your hands, then roughly chop. Bring a pan of water to the boil, add the sugar snap peas, let them cook for two minutes, then remove and drain.

Bring a large, deep pan of water to the boil, salt it generously, cook the bucatini or other thin pasta for about nine minutes or until just tender, then drain.

Cut the courgette into thick slices, then into quarters. Melt the butter in a shallow pan and add a couple of tablespoons of olive oil. Fry the courgette for four or five minutes till it starts to colour, then add the spinach and cooked sugar snaps. Roughly chop the parsley and add to the vegetables.

Pour the double cream into the vegetables and combine gently. Let it simmer for a minute, then pour the mixture over the drained pasta and toss together gently. Pass a bowl of grated Parmesan around at the table.

(continued)

• The spinach needs to be cooked as briefly as possible. A bowl of water and ice cubes is then a useful thing in which to plunge the steamed spinach, helping to retain its bright colour before wringing it almost, but not completely dry.

• You could use a narrow ribbon pasta such as fettucine instead of the bucatini. There is only enough cream in the recipe to coat the pasta – if you use a shape such as orecchiette or conchiglie, one that will hold sauce, then use a little more cream. An addition of tomatoes, quartered or roughly chopped, is tempting.

On the hob   227

CAULIFLOWER, PUMPKIN SEEDS, BREADCRUMBS

Crisp fried cauliflower. A soft creamy purée. The toothsome crunch of toasted seeds.

Serves 2–3

vegetable stock 500ml
cauliflower 1kg
olive oil
fresh white breadcrumbs 50g

parsley leaves 10g
pumpkin seeds 3 tablespoons
fresh horseradish 1 tablespoon

Bring the vegetable stock to the boil in a medium-sized saucepan. Trim the cauliflower, then cut into 'steaks' about 2cm thick. Lower these into the boiling stock, then reduce the heat so that the stock simmers. Partially cover the pan with a lid and leave to cook till the cauliflower is soft enough to pierce effortlessly with a skewer – a matter of fifteen minutes or so.

While the cauliflower cooks, warm three tablespoons of olive oil in a shallow pan, then add the breadcrumbs and cook till golden, constantly stirring and tossing so they colour evenly. Roughly chop the parsley and pumpkin seeds, and fold into the breadcrumbs with the horseradish. Season with salt and pepper and set aside.

Blend half the cauliflower steaks to a smooth cream in a blender or food processor with approximately half the hot stock, seasoning as you go.

Warm a glug or two of olive oil in a frying pan, lower in the reserved, cooked cauliflower slices, carefully drained, and fry till golden. Gently turn and cook the other side till lightly crisp around the edges. They may fall apart a little, no matter. Divide the cauliflower purée between two plates, slip the fried cauliflower on top, then season with the crumbs and seeds.

• Keeping the slices of cauliflower on the thick side will help the slices hold together. The pieces that stand proud of the stock and cook in the

(continued)

steam are the ones to fry. Those that cook under the liquid are the ones to purée. They will absorb some of the flavours of your stock.

• Snippets of crisp bacon, pancetta or pork crackling could be introduced to the breadcrumb and parsley crumble. A trickle of cream and a handful of grated Pecorino would be a worthwhile addition to the cauliflower purée. The sauce, topped with a little grated Parmesan, could be spooned over the cauliflower and grilled, to give a toasted crust.

On the hob 231

CAULIFLOWER, GARLIC, SPICES

A soothing cream. A spicy crunch.

Serves 2

cauliflower 600g
milk 500ml
bay leaves 3
half a nutmeg
garlic 3 cloves
groundnut or vegetable oil
    4 tablespoons
butter 70g

coriander leaves a small
    handful, chopped

For the spice mix:
coriander seeds ½ teaspoon
cumin seeds 1 teaspoon
chilli flakes ½ teaspoon
ground ginger ½ teaspoon

Remove three-quarters of the cauliflower florets from their stalks and set aside. Cut the remainder of the cauliflower into large pieces and put them in a deep saucepan, pour over the milk, tuck in the bay leaves and add the nutmeg. Bring to the boil, then lower the heat and leave to simmer for about fifteen minutes until the cauliflower is completely tender.

Grind the coriander seeds to powder then mix with the cumin seeds, chilli flakes and ground ginger. Peel and thinly slice the garlic. Warm the oil in a shallow pan, add the garlic and let it colour lightly, then introduce the spices and the reserved cauliflower. Cover with a lid and cook for five minutes until the cauliflower has started to brown a little.

Drain the boiled cauliflower, discarding the aromatics but keeping the milk, and process to a cream in a blender or food processor, using enough of the milk to give a soft purée. Season to taste, then spoon into shallow dishes. Check the seasoning of the fried cauliflower too, adding salt if necessary (it should be quite spicy as it will be eaten with the soft, mild purée).

Divide the cauliflower and garlic between the dishes of purée, add a little coriander to each and serve.

FETTUCINE, SAMPHIRE, LEMON

A taste of the seashore.

Serves 2

fettucine 200g
olive oil 4 tablespoons
a fat clove of young, fresh garlic

samphire 150g
crème fraîche 200g
a lemon

Put a large, deep pot of water on to boil, then salt it generously. As the water reaches the boil, add the fettucine. Cook until just tender, about two minutes less than the time on the packet.

In a small frying pan, warm the olive oil. Slice the garlic very thinly, add it to the pan, then let it cook to a deep golden brown. Remove from the pan, reserving a little of the garlic oil, and let it drain on kitchen paper. Wash the samphire in cold water and shake it dry.

When the fettucine is cooked, drain and return to the pan, toss with the samphire, then transfer to bowls or plates. Divide the crème fraîche between the bowls, scatter over the garlic and a little of its oil, then finely grate the lemon zest over the top. Freshen with a tiny squeeze of lemon juice.

FREEKEH, AVOCADO, CHIVES

Chewy, nutty grains. The crunch of cucumber.

Serves 2

freekeh 150g	chickpeas 1 × 400g can
cucumber 180g	chives roughly 2 tablespoons,
an avocado, ripe but firm	chopped
olive oil 2 tablespoons	balsamic vinegar 1 teaspoon
ras el hanout 2 teaspoons	juice of half a lemon

Put a pan of water on to boil. Rinse the freekeh in cold water, then add to the boiling water and leave to cook for fifteen to twenty-five minutes till tender but slightly chewy. Drain and set aside.

Peel the cucumber, halve lengthways and discard the seeds, then cut the flesh into small dice. Halve, stone and peel the avocado, then cut into small cubes.

Warm the olive oil in a shallow pan, add the ras el hanout and let it warm through (it is already roasted, so a minute or two over heat is long enough). Add the cooked and drained freekeh and the rinsed chickpeas, together with a little salt. When the chickpeas are hot, stir in the cucumber, chives and avocado. Stir gently; you don't want to crush the avocado. Trickle over the balsamic vinegar and a squeeze of lemon, to taste, and serve.

• Freekeh is whole roasted wheat. It can take anything from fifteen to twenty-five minutes to reach the point where it is nutty and enjoyably chewy. I find it best to salt it after cooking rather than adding salt to the cooking water, which seems, sometimes, to toughen it.
• All manner of grains can be substituted for the freekeh, such as barley or rye, but the cooking times will vary according to which grain you choose. Whole grains such as pot barley will take longer to cook than pearl barley.

(continued)

• Use this salad as a base for adding other ingredients, such as chopped tomatoes, mint, spring onions. You can add feta or grated ricotta salata, the aged, salted sheep's cheese, if you wish. I sometimes add lemon juice to the warm dressing.

POTATOES, WILD GARLIC

Earthy new potatoes. Mild, sweet garlic. Soothing cream.

Serves 3–4, as a side dish

new potatoes 450g
butter 20g
garlic leaves 85g

double cream 250ml
lemon juice 1 teaspoon
lemon zest 1 teaspoon

Scrub the new potatoes, but do not peel them. Either steam them in a colander over boiling water covered with a lid or boil them in lightly salted water. They will need 8–15 minutes depending on their size.

Melt the butter in a saucepan, add the garlic leaves and let them cook for a minute or two, turning them in the butter as they soften. Once they have wilted, pour in the cream, then bring to the boil. As the cream starts to boil, remove quickly from the heat, season lightly with pepper, cover and set aside for ten minutes to infuse.

Drain the potatoes and put them on a large serving plate. Using the back of a spoon or a potato masher, press firmly down to lightly crush them. Ideally, the skins should be broken and the flesh open enough to take up the dressing, but not so heavily crushed they fall to pieces.

Add the lemon juice and zest to the cream, then spoon the softened garlic leaves and sauce over the potatoes, leave for a few minutes for the cream to soak in, and eat whilst still hot.

• If garlic leaves prove evasive, use six cloves of new, wet garlic instead, each clove crushed flat and left in the hot cream for fifteen minutes to infuse, and remove them before you pour the cream over the potatoes. I add pepper too, but not salt, which I already added to the potato cooking water.

PEAS, PAPPARDELLE, PARMESAN

Quiet flavours.

Serves 2

vegetable stock 600ml
peas 300g (podded weight)
pappardelle 300g

Parmesan 25g, grated
fresh young sheep's or
   goat's cheese 200g

Put the vegetable stock on to boil (you can use water at a push). Keeping a handful of raw peas to one side, cook the rest in the boiling stock for five to seven minutes, depending on their size. Whilst the peas cook, boil the pappardelle for seven to eight minutes in generously salted water.

Put the peas and 150ml of their cooking liquor into a blender and process till smooth, introducing more stock as necessary to produce a thin, brightly flavoured sauce. Drain the pasta and return to the pan, pour in the pea sauce, scatter over the Parmesan and fold in. Check the seasoning. Divide between two deep plates.

Break the sheep's cheese into large pieces, scatter over the pasta with the reserved raw peas and serve.

• Start the pea sauce before putting the pasta on. The sauce will hold in good condition whilst the pasta cooks. If you are using fresh peas, check them every minute or so throughout cooking; they can take anything from four minutes to much longer to become tender. Much depends on their age and size. If you are using frozen peas, they should be done in four to five minutes. Process the peas and their stock in two goes rather than risk overfilling the blender. (Sorry. Obvious, I know, but it is so easy to.)
• You can make a similar sauce with broad beans. They are more starchy than peas, so be prepared to add a little more vegetable stock during blending.

NEW POTATOES, GARLIC, PEPPERS

The ease of a traybake. The earthy warmth of potatoes.

Serves 2

Romano peppers 3
round 'bell' pepper 1 yellow or red
garlic 4 cloves
new potatoes 700g

olive oil 8 tablespoons
vegetable or chicken stock 300ml
spring onions 3

Slice the Romano peppers in half from shoulder to tip. Cut the 'bell' pepper into quarters and remove the seeds and any white core. Peel and flatten the garlic. Thinly slice the potatoes.

Warm the olive oil in a large frying pan or flameproof casserole and add all the peppers, letting them cook over a moderate heat for five minutes, covered with a lid, until they relax. Remove the peppers with a slotted spoon, leaving the oil intact in the pan, and set aside.

Add the garlic and the potatoes to the pan, cooking them in one layer if possible. When they are golden underneath, turn over and lightly colour the other side. Return the peppers to the pan, season with salt and pepper, mix the ingredients together, then pour over the chicken or vegetable stock and bring to the boil.

Lower the heat and leave to simmer, partially covered by a lid. After eight minutes or so, check the potatoes for softness: they should be tender and easy to crush. Turn and cook the other side. Continue cooking until all is golden and soft, the potatoes are a little broken up and there is a good layer of sweet, garlic-scented juice. Chop the spring onions and scatter them in at the last minute, letting them briefly soften before serving.

• Give the peppers plenty of time to soften and sweeten. The caramelised juices are integral to the dish. Keeping the ingredients covered as they cook is crucial so they partly fry, partly steam. *(continued)*

• Try sweet potatoes. The cooking time needs to be lessened somewhat, and the potatoes crumble more, but their sweetness is a thoroughly good thing with which to accompany a roast.

On the hob   247

SUMMER SQUASH, TOMATOES, SPINACH

The bounty of late summer, lightly spiced.

Serves 4

onions 3 medium
groundnut or vegetable oil
   3 tablespoons
yellow mustard seeds 2 teaspoons
ground turmeric 2 teaspoons
ground cumin 2 teaspoons
ground cayenne ½ teaspoon
cherry tomatoes 350g
round summer squash or
   courgettes 600g
spinach with stalks 350g
chickpeas 1 × 400g can

Peel the onions, halve them, then cut each half into three or four segments. Warm the oil in a large, heavy-based casserole, add the yellow mustard seeds and cook for a minute, then, as they start to pop, stir in the onions, turmeric, cumin and cayenne and lower the heat. Cook for fifteen minutes, partially covering the pan with a lid and stirring occasionally.

When the onions are golden and fragrant, halve the cherry tomatoes, add them to the onions and leave to cook until soft. Cut the squash into thick segments, or courgettes into thick slices roughly the length of a wine cork. Fold them into the onions and tomatoes, together with 200ml of water, and bring to the boil. Leave the stew simmering for fifteen minutes.

Wash the spinach and remove the toughest of the stalks. Put the wet leaves into a non-stick pan with a lid and cook them for a minute or two over a moderate heat, letting the leaves steam and relax. Remove them from the pan, then cool immediately under cold running water and drain.

Drain and rinse the chickpeas and stir them into the onions. Continue cooking, stirring from time to time, until the courgettes are translucent and tender. Check the seasoning – you may want to add salt. Squeeze as much water as possible from the spinach, then fold into the courgettes gently and without crushing them. And serve.

TOMATOES, CHICKPEAS, CASHEWS

The sweet-sharp savour of summer tomatoes. The crunch of cashews.

Serves 2

garlic 2 cloves
ginger a 40g knob
small hot chilli 1
groundnut oil 2 tablespoons
yellow mustard seeds
   2 teaspoons
tomatoes 400g

onions 2
olive oil 2 tablespoons
cumin seeds 1 teaspoon
cashew nuts 50g
chickpeas 1 × 400g can
coriander leaves a handful,
   chopped

Peel and thinly slice the garlic. Peel the ginger and cut it into matchsticks. Finely chop the chilli. Warm the groundnut oil in a saucepan, add the garlic, ginger and chilli and fry for a couple of minutes over a moderate heat, until the garlic is pale gold.

Stir in the yellow mustard seeds. Let them cook for a minute or two. Roughly chop the tomatoes, stir them in, then leave to cook for fifteen minutes, giving it the occasional stir.

Peel the onions, halve them, then cut into thick segments. Cook them in the olive oil until soft, then add the cumin seeds and cashew nuts. Fry till the onions are soft and deep gold in colour.

Drain and rinse the chickpeas and stir into the tomato sauce. Season carefully, then, when piping hot, divide between two bowls. Spoon the onions and cashews on top and serve, if you wish, with a little coriander stirred through at the last minute.

TOMATOES, COURGETTES, PEAS

Summer stew.

Serves 2

garlic   2 cloves
olive oil   1 tablespoon
cumin seeds   2 teaspoons
tomatoes   500g
ground chilli, mild or hot
   1 teaspoon
ground turmeric   1 teaspoon

broad beans   500g (weight with
   pods)
courgettes or summer squash   350g
sugar snap peas   150g
peas, podded or frozen   a couple
   of handfuls
cherry tomatoes   150g

Peel and crush the garlic. Put the olive oil in a shallow-sided pan and fry the garlic for a minute or so till fragrant, then stir in the cumin seeds. Chop the tomatoes and add them to the pan. Stir in the chilli, turmeric and a generous seasoning of salt and black pepper. Let the tomatoes and spices cook for fifteen to twenty minutes or so, until you have a soft, sauce-like texture and much spicy juice.

Meanwhile, pod the broad beans and cook them briefly in boiling water. Drain and, if they are large, squeeze them from their thin, pale skins. Roughly chop the courgettes or summer squash and add them to the tomatoes. As the courgettes start to soften, slice the sugar snaps and stir them in, together with the cooked beans. Add the peas and continue cooking for a few minutes until the peas are almost tender.

Five minutes before serving, add the cherry tomatoes, halved, and let them soften but not lose their shape. Check the seasoning – it should be mildly spicy – and serve.

TROFIE, PARSLEY, PECORINO

The verdant green of parsley. The warmth of fresh horseradish.

Serves 2

trofie or other small pasta 200g
butter 50g
grated fresh horseradish 15–20g

Pecorino 50g, finely grated
parsley, chopped 3 tablespoons

Bring a large, deep pot of water to the boil, salt generously and add the trofie. When the pasta is tender, about nine to twelve minutes depending on how firm you like it, drain lightly and return immediately to the empty pan. Add the butter in small pieces and the grated horseradish, Pecorino and parsley. Check the seasoning and serve on shallow plates.

• The most simple and pleasing of suppers – hot pasta, grated cheese, chopped herbs tossed with butter and finely grated horseradish root. A dish that relies on sweet, pale butter, young, crisp horseradish and the freshest parsley. Don't even think of using horseradish from a jar.

PUDDING

Not every meal needs to end with something sweet, but it is rarely a bad idea. In high summer, a wedge of watermelon, a perfect peach or a bowl of raspberries will often do. Such seasonal treasure needs little embellishment. I will slice a peach or ripe apricot into a glass of sweet, very cold wine; tip a handful of raspberries into a glass of prosecco or pour a small, intense espresso over a ball of vanilla ice cream, but sometimes even that isn't enough.

Summer fruits cry out for dairy and pastry, for cake and for meringue. A shop-bought meringue can be crushed with whipped cream and summer fruits, it can be trickled with a dark and sharp fruit purée or sandwiched with sliced peaches and crushed raspberries. A slice of plain cake, a good one, from a pâtisserie is all you need to accompany greengages or plums that have been roasted with a little honey and are served with a jug of cream. Pastry too: a pie seems just a little too much trouble for a midweek dinner, which is after all the heart and soul of this book, yet a sweet shortcrust can be made in minutes in a food processor and need only go on top, rather than under the fruit. We are not talking about finely honed pâtisserie here, just a soft crust to work with sweet, dark cherries or apricots and thirty minutes of your time.

There are many occasions when I am happy to make pastry by hand, to roll it out on a floured board, push it carefully into a tart tin and bake it blind using baking beans. To make a pastry cream for filling it, then add artfully arranged fruit. It's a faff, but also a calm way to spend an hour or two on a cool spring day. But on a hot summer's day I am just as content with a tart base that requires no more than ten minutes' work. A shortbread mix made from flour, butter and ground nuts (almonds, hazelnuts, pistachios), made in seconds in the food processor, pressed into a disc, baked, then loaded with ripe berries. You have the seasonal marriage of a crisp crust and fruit, yet brought together with little effort.

I see no reason why a hot pudding need be ruled out just because the sun is high in the sky. Not that anyone fancies jam roly-poly on a summer's afternoon, but the warm, heady juices of a hot summer pudding, its layers of bread and fruit baked in the oven and served with cream, are certainly on my list of good things. A pastry made from baked croissants, split and topped with ripe apricots and honey; a plum pie whose crust is not pastry but made from crumbly cookie dough; an almond crumble hiding small plums or green-gages; a mix of summer berries cooked on the hob with a sprinkling of sugar and a little water till the berries start to burst and flood the pan with deep purple juices.

I have included a water ice here, which barely fits into the admittedly loose structure of this book. But it is a water ice that can be made in minutes, doesn't need any specialist equipment and is, frankly, a doddle. On a baking hot summer's day, after dinner outside, I cannot think of many things I would rather eat.

PLUMS, CROISSANTS

Honey-sweet plums, flaking crumbs.

Makes 4

croissants 2	honey 4 tablespoons
plums, medium-sized, ripe 6	rosemary, chopped 2 teaspoons

Slice the croissants in half horizontally and place them cut side up on a baking sheet. Toast them lightly under an oven grill.

Halve and stone the plums and place three halves, skin side down, on each slice of croissant. Warm the honey and chopped rosemary in a small pan, then trickle over the plums and croissants, letting it collect in the hollows of the fruit.

Place under a hot grill, not too close to the heat, for about five minutes, or in an oven at 180°C/Gas 4 for fifteen to twenty minutes till the croissant is crisp and there are little pools of honey bubbling on the surface of the fruit.

• Should your croissants be particularly plump, remove a thin slice from the crown of each with a knife so it sits level on the baking sheet, otherwise your plums will topple and your honey will be spilled.
• The cooking time is too brief to coax an under-ripe plum into melting, spoon-soft submission. It is truly not worth making this with anything but the very ripest of fruit. The sort that glow as if illuminated from within.
• Without croissants, thick white toast will be welcome here, as might slices of sweet cake-like brioche.
• A small jug of double cream would be in order here.

BLACKBERRY, APPLE, MARZIPAN

Soft apples, mildly spiced. A crumble crust that is soft, buttery and comforting. The merest hint of festivity.

Serves 6

For the filling:
sharp apples 900g
butter 20g
caster sugar 2 tablespoons
unfiltered apple juice 100ml
a pinch of ground cinnamon
blackberries 200g

For the crumble:
butter 90g
plain flour 150g
ground almonds 5 tablespoons
marzipan 100g
flaked almonds a small handful

To serve: double cream or soured cream

Peel, quarter and core the apples then cut each piece into four segments. Melt the butter in a shallow pan over a moderate heat, add the apples and sugar and let them cook for ten minutes or so, turning occasionally, until the fruit is pale gold and approaching tenderness. Stir in the juice, sprinkle over the cinnamon, tip in the blackberries and set aside. Set the oven at 180°C/Gas 4.

Make the crumble: rub the butter into the flour, either using your fingertips or a food processor, until you have fine crumbs. Fold in the ground almonds. Tear the marzipan into small cubes, about 2cm in size, and stir into the crumble.

Transfer the fruit to a deep baking dish approximately 22 × 24cm. Loosely scatter the crumble over the top, then the flaked almonds. Bake for fifty minutes to an hour until the crumble is golden and a little of the fruit has bled temptingly into the crust here and there. Leave to calm down for ten minutes or so before serving, if you wish, with double or soured cream. *(continued)*

• Twisting nuggets of marzipan from the block with your fingers, rather than cutting them into neat dice with a knife, will give a more interesting texture as they soften into the crumble crust.

• The recipe can be speeded up by omitting to pre-cook the apples, but doing so risks a less juicy and fluffy filling.

• Blueberries would make an admirable, if slightly sweeter, substitute for the blackberries.

BLACKCURRANT, YOGHURT

Mercifully non-sweet. Clean-tasting. Bright as a button.

Serves 4

blackcurrants, fresh or
frozen 125g

raspberries 125g
natural yoghurt 500g

Put the blackcurrants and raspberries in a bowl and crush them lightly with a fork or a potato masher. Fold in the yoghurt, stirring only enough to send a purple ripple of colour through the pure white yoghurt.

Divide between four small freezerproof dishes, cover each with clingfilm and freeze for one and half to two hours till lightly, but not completely frozen.

• The dessert is at its most enticing when the surface and outer edge of the yoghurt is lightly frosted and the centre is still creamy. It is worth checking progress regularly with a skewer.

• If the desserts are left to freeze fully, leave them at room temperature for half an hour or so before serving. They should be eaten when soft enough to submit to light pressure from a teaspoon.

CHERRY, SWEET PASTRY

A soft, tender crust for a plate of cherries, berries or plums.

Serves 6

For the pastry:
plain flour 230g
butter 140g
icing sugar 50g
a large egg yolk
a little beaten egg to seal and
      glaze the pie

For the filling:
cherries 800g
blueberries 200g
cornflour 3 tablespoons
a lemon
caster sugar 100g, plus a
      little extra

You will need a wide-rimmed metal pie plate or tart tin measuring approximately 26cm in diameter (including rim).

Make the pastry: put the flour into the bowl of a food processor, cut the butter into pieces and add to the bowl, then process till the ingredients resemble fine, fresh breadcrumbs. Mix in the icing sugar and the egg yolk. Transfer the mixture to a bowl, then bring the dough together with your hands to form a smooth ball. Wrap in baking parchment or clingfilm and refrigerate for twenty minutes.

Stone the cherries, put them in a mixing bowl, then add the blueberries and the cornflour. Finely grate the lemon zest, add it to the fruit, then cut the lemon in half and squeeze the juice. Sprinkle the juice over the fruit and add the sugar. Tumble the fruit, cornflour, juice, zest and sugar together and set aside.

Place an empty baking sheet in the oven, then preheat to 200°C/Gas 6. Cut the pastry in half. Roll out one half to fit the base of the pie plate or tin, then lower into the tin, leaving any overhanging pastry in place. Spoon the filling into the tin, leaving a bare rim of pastry around the edge. Brush the rim with a little beaten egg.   *(continued)*

Roll out the remaining pastry and place over the top of the tart, pressing firmly around the rim to seal. Trim the pastry. Brush the surface with beaten egg, pierce a small hole in the middle to let out any steam, then sprinkle the pie lightly with caster sugar. Bake for 25–30 minutes, on the heated baking sheet, till golden.

• The crust is made in five minutes in a food processor, and not much longer should you prefer to do it by hand. The pastry is fragile in the extreme and its shortbread-like tenderness can be used with apricots, plums and berries too.

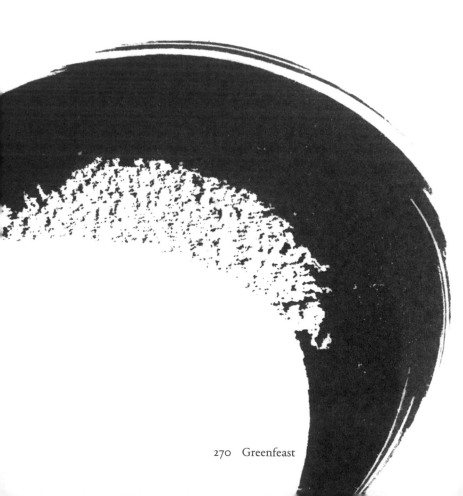

LEMON RICE, MANGO, ICE CREAM

The contrast of creamy rice, mango purée, cold ice cream. Warm, yet refreshing.

Serves 4

lemon grass stalks 4 large
creamy milk 500ml
pudding rice 150g
caster sugar (or palm sugar if
    possible) 1 tablespoon

mangoes, small, ripe 2
vanilla ice cream 4 scoops
a lemon

Using a heavy rolling pin or pestle, smash the lemon grass stalks, keeping them intact but in large splinters. Put them in a saucepan, then pour in the milk and 500ml of water. Bring to the boil, then remove from the heat, cover tightly with a lid, and let the liquid infuse with the lemon grass for half an hour.

Pour the milk through a sieve into a clean saucepan, add the rice and bring to the boil. Lower the heat to a simmer and leave to cook for about twenty-five minutes, stirring regularly, until the grains are soft and plump. Should they take longer, top up the liquid with a little boiling water. Towards the end of the cooking time, add the sugar.

Peel the mangoes and cut the flesh from the stone, then purée in a blender or food processor. Spoon the rice into dishes, add a pool of mango purée, then a ball of vanilla ice cream. Finely grate the lemon zest over the rice and ice cream.

Let the ice cream soften in the warm rice as you eat.

• If your rice is taking longer than twenty-five minutes, keep the heat at a low to moderate simmer, stir in a little boiling water from the kettle and continue cooking, stirring often, till tender.
• One for the Alphonso mango season in June and July.

CUCUMBER, BASIL, CREAM CHEESE

A soft, savoury cheesecake for a summer's day.

Serves 6–8

For the base:
cheese oatcakes 100g
rice crackers 120g

For the filling:
cucumber 375g
basil 12g
mint leaves 10g
tarragon vinegar 1 tablespoon
cream cheese 500g
ricotta 250g

Work the oatcakes and rice crackers to crumbs in a food processor or using a plastic bag and a rolling pin. Use most of the crumbs to line the base of a 20cm round, springform or loose-bottomed cake tin. Chill in the refrigerator.

Coarsely grate the cucumber into a colander, sprinkle generously with salt, then leave to drain.

Finely chop the basil and mint, put them in a mixing bowl, then add the tarragon vinegar. Fold in the cream cheese and ricotta. Squeeze the cucumber in your hands to remove any excess water, then mix with the herbed cream cheese, adding a few twists of black pepper.

Scoop the filling into the chilled cake tin, lightly smoothing the top with the back of a spoon. Press the reserved crumbs around the edge, cover with a plate or clingfilm and refrigerate for two hours. Release the cake from its tin and serve.

FIG, GOAT'S CHEESE, HONEY

A crisp parcel of warm goat's cheese, honey, figs and thyme. Redolent of a provincial French market in late summer.

Serves 2–4

butter 100–150g
pine kernels 4 teaspoons
figs, small 8
filo pastry 4 sheets measuring
    30 × 22cm

goat's cheese 4 × 75g pieces
honey 4 heaped teaspoons
thyme leaves 2 teaspoons
thyme sprigs 4

Place a baking sheet or pizza stone in the oven and set the heat to 200°C/ Gas 6.

Melt the butter in a small saucepan and set aside. Toast the pine kernels in a dry pan. Slice each fig horizontally into four rounds.

Lay one sheet of pastry flat on a chopping board, longest edge towards you, then cut in half to give two pieces measuring 15 × 22cm. Brush one half generously with some of the warm, melted butter, then scatter over a teaspoon of the toasted pine kernels.

Place the other half sheet on top and brush it with more melted butter. Lay a piece of goat's cheese in the middle of the pastry, add two of the sliced figs, a teaspoon of the honey and half a teaspoon of the thyme leaves. Bring the sides of the pastry together, folding the edges to make a parcel, as neatly or as randomly as you wish. Press the buttered edges together tightly to seal.

Continue with the remaining pastry, pine kernels, cheese, figs, honey and herbs, making four parcels in all. Place them on a baking sheet, put the thyme sprigs on top, brush with more butter, place the baking sheet on top of the preheated pizza stone or metal baking sheet and bake for about ten to fifteen minutes till crisp. *(continued)*

Remove the pastries from the oven, then brush with any remaining butter, and, if you wish, a little more honey.

• The undercrust of the parcels will be all the crisper for being baked on top of a hot pizza stone or extra baking sheet. Without it, your parcels will suffer the indignity of a soggy bottom.

• Sealing the edges as tightly as possible will prevent any leaking honey or molten cheese, though they are likely to ooze a little however tenaciously you seal the parcels.

• Offer one per person after a meal, or two for a light supper or lunch, perhaps with a salad of bitter leaves. Try red chicory to echo the figs, watercress or frisée, dressed with olive oil, lemon juice and parsley.

CURRANTS, GIN, BREAD

Summer pudding, but served hot, in all its heady, scarlet-mauve glory.

Serves 6

redcurrants and blackcurrants
   500g
raspberries 350g
caster sugar 125g, plus 3 tablespoons

sloe gin 100ml
white bread, sliced 400g
a little icing sugar and double
   cream to finish

Pull the currants from their stalks and put them in a stainless steel or enamelled saucepan with the raspberries, caster sugar and 375ml of water. Place the pan over a moderate heat and bring to the boil. Lower the heat and leave to simmer for seven to ten minutes or until the berries start to burst and the sugar has dissolved. Pour in the sloe gin and remove from the heat.

Set the oven at 200°C/Gas 6. Remove any particularly chewy crusts from the bread. You can leave any softer ones in place or cut them off as you wish. Place the bread in a shallow baking dish, approximately 22cm in diameter, arranging the slices uniformly or hugger-mugger as the fancy takes you. Spoon the berries and their juice over the bread, making sure that it is completely soaked with purple juice.

Scatter 3 tablespoons of sugar over the surface and bake for twenty-five minutes till the juices are bubbling and the top is lightly crisp in places. Dust with icing sugar if you wish and serve hot with double cream.

• The sloe gin is an option. The flavour is not immediately apparent. Its addition lends a deep, mellow fruitiness to the proceedings, intensifying the flavours of the berries. I should add that we ate half and had the remainder next day, for breakfast, with a ribbon of sheep's yoghurt over it so no one could accuse us having pudding for breakfast.

MERINGUE, APRICOTS, BLACKCURRANTS

Crisp white wafers of sugar, billowing folds of cream, piquant fruits.

Serves 4

apricots 8
sugar 5 tablespoons
blackcurrants 400g

double cream 250ml
meringues 200g

Halve and stone the apricots and put them in a saucepan with 3 tablespoons of the sugar and 100ml of water. Bring to the boil, then lower the heat and leave to simmer until the fruit is tender enough to crush, effortlessly, with your thumb and fingers. The softer and silkier the fruit, the better. Remove from the heat and leave to cool.

Pull the blackcurrants from their stalks, then let them cook in a small pan with the remaining sugar and 100ml of water until the berries start to burst.

Whip the cream in a large mixing bowl till thick enough to sit in soft waves. Crumble the meringues into large pieces, dropping them into the cream. Lift the apricots from their syrup and put into the meringue and cream, then spoon over the blackcurrants and a little of their deep purple juice.

• The syrups, devoid of their fruits, can be chilled overnight in the fridge and served with strained yoghurt for breakfast.
• I like to keep the meringue pieces on the large side, so they form a crisp contrast with the whipped cream and soft, warm fruits. Small pieces tend to dissolve into the cream.

PEACH, BLACKBERRIES, ICE CREAM

An ice-cream slice whose flavours are reminiscent of summer days on the beach, cornet in hand.

Serves 8

Japanese black sesame rice cakes 50g
blackberries 125g
shelled pistachios 50g
ripe peaches 2, medium
vanilla ice cream 1 litre

You will need a rectangular cake tin, measuring roughly 20 × 12cm, lined with clingfilm and with enough hanging over the sides to cover the top.

Roughly crush the rice cakes to the size of coarse gravel and put in a bowl. (A plastic bag and a rolling pin are extremely handy for this. A food processor is too brutal.) Cut each blackberry in half and add to the rice cakes.

Roughly chop the pistachios. Halve, stone and dice the peaches, then fold into the crumbs together with the pistachios. Let the ice cream soften, but not melt, then scoop into the crumbs, nuts and fruit. Fold everything lightly together, taking care not to crush the fruit. There is something delightful about the way the blackberries bleed a little into the ice cream.

Press the ice cream mixture into the lined cake tin, fold the clingfilm over the surface, then place in the freezer for at least four hours. Serve in slices no thicker than a finger. A large knife, its blade warmed with hot water from the kettle, will be of help here.

• The Clearspring brand of square rice cakes is perfect for this, being especially light and airy. Use the more easily accessible 'ceiling tile' variety if that is all that is available.
• Fold the ingredients together lightly. Seeing the pistachios, rice cake crumbs and blackberries rippled through the ice cream like a road map

(continued)

is more pleasing than when the ingredients are crushed and the parfait turned pink by too enthusiastic a mixing.

• If you let the parfait completely harden in the freezer, it is best to let it thaw for a good half an hour before slicing. No one wants to hack away at their dessert.

PLUMS, BROWN SUGAR, HAZELNUTS

Late summer fruit baked under a soft and crumbly cookie crust.

Serves 4

butter 90g
soft brown sugar 90g
caster sugar 90g
vanilla extract a couple of drops
an egg

plain flour 150g
hazelnuts 2 tablespoons,
    roughly chopped
plums 800g

Set the oven at 200°C/Gas 6. Put the butter in the bowl of a food mixer, add the sugars and beat till pale and fluffy. Add a couple of drops of vanilla extract and a pinch of salt. Break the egg into a small bowl and beat lightly with a fork, then add to the butter and sugar, beating continuously. With the beater still turning, add the flour and the hazelnuts. Turn the mixture out onto a floured board.

Halve and stone the plums and pack them into a deep-sided baking dish about 22cm in diameter. Pat the cookie dough into a thick disc large enough to cover the dish, then place on top of the plums.

Bake for 45 minutes, or until the surface is lightly crisp and the plum juices are peeping through. Eat warm, with cream, custard or yoghurt.

• The crust is fragile. It is easiest to lift the raw dough into place by sliding the loose base of a tart tin under the patted-out dough and pushing it gently into place. You can patch any tears once the dough is on top of the fruit. No worries should your dough crumble. The plum juice will bubble enticingly through any cracks.
• Plums are just one possible fruit here – any gages or damsons will work brilliantly too – but it is best to avoid anything too sweet. The cookie dough provides all the sweetness you need.

SPONGE FINGERS, CHERRY, CUSTARD

Much creamy softness here, but with a light, refreshing note at its base that prevents it cloying.

Serves 6

sponge fingers or trifle
   sponges 100g
orange juice 400ml
apricot jam 5 tablespoons
Grand Marnier, Cointreau or
   sherry 3–4 tablespoons

fresh, ripe cherries 400g
ready-made vanilla custard
   400g
double cream 250ml

Break the sponge fingers into a deep serving dish about 19–20cm in diameter. Pour the orange juice into a small saucepan, add the jam and the alcohol and warm over a moderate heat, removing as soon as the jam has melted. Pour the hot mixture over the sponge, pressing down lightly with your spoon to make sure the pieces are fully soaked. Set aside to cool.

Halve and stone the cherries. Scatter half the cherries over the sponge. Spoon the custard over the cherries, smooth flat, then refrigerate for an hour.

Whip the cream till thick, but not so much that it will stand in peaks. It should sit in soft folds, just managing to keep its shape on the whisk. Spread the cream gently over the custard. Refrigerate for several hours. Finish with the reserved cherries.

• The quality of ready-made custard varies enormously. I prefer the premium varieties sold in plastic tubs from the chilled cabinet in the supermarket: the soft, yellow sauces made with eggs, cream and vanilla – you will need to check the ingredients. The budget-priced and low-fat varieties are thin, over-sweet and lack the essential sensuality needed for a trifle. *(continued)*

• The exact texture of the cream is crucial. May I suggest you whip it to the point where the cream slouches, rather than sits up straight.

• An overnight sleep in the fridge, tightly covered with clingfilm, will improve your trifle. Patience will out.

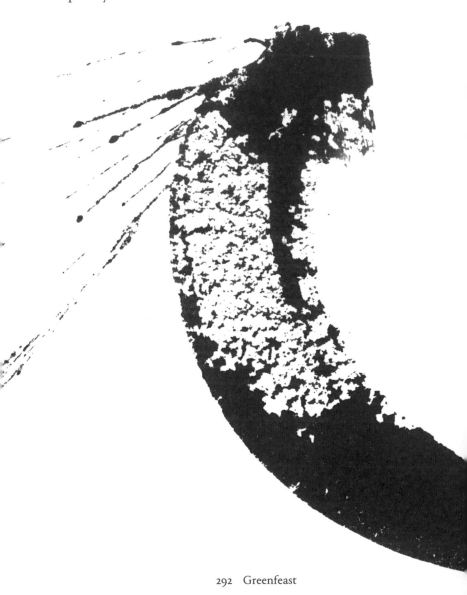

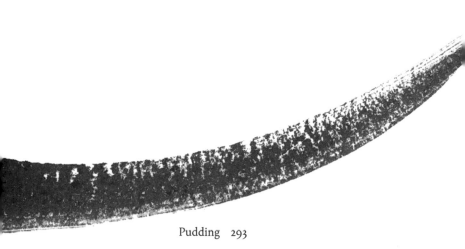

Pudding   293

PLUMS, CLOVES, BAY

Glowing, lightly sugared and spiced fruits for dessert or breakfast.

Serves 4

plums (or apricots) 750g
caster sugar 4 tablespoons
  (to taste)

cloves 4
half a cinnamon stick
bay leaves 3

Halve and stone the fruit, dropping it into a saucepan as you go. Add the sugar and six tablespoons of water, cloves, cinnamon and bay, then bring to the boil.

Lower the heat and let the fruit simmer gently for a good ten to twenty minutes depending on its ripeness. Remove from the heat once it is soft and easy to crush with the back of a spoon. Pour into a bowl and set aside to cool a little.

• Jolly useful for adding tart juices to a mess of crumbled meringue and whipped cream.
• The deep amber-red juice is a good thing to find in your fridge too. I spoon it, in long, sticky rivulets, over my breakfast yoghurt.

RICOTTA, ORANGE BLOSSOM, CHERRIES

A fresh, light cream for cherries or berries. Ten minutes of actual hands-on cooking. Then a little patience.

Serves 4

ricotta 250g	finely grated orange zest
mascarpone 250g	2 teaspoons
a medium-sized orange	*For the compote:*
vanilla extract ½–1 teaspoon	blackcurrants 75g
orange blossom water 1 teaspoon	cherries 250g
icing sugar, to taste	caster sugar 1 tablespoon

Put the ricotta and mascarpone into a mixing bowl. Finely grate the zest from the orange and stir it in, together with the vanilla extract and orange blossom water to taste.

Line a small sieve or colander with a piece of clean muslin (a new, fresh-from-the-packet J-cloth will do) and spoon the ricotta cream into it. Suspend the sieve over a bowl so there is room for any whey to run off, then cover the surface with a piece of clingfilm and a weight and small, heavy plate, then refrigerate for at least four hours.

Make the compote: top and tail the blackcurrants and put them in a stainless steel saucepan. (They will 'react' with aluminium.) Stone the cherries, add them to the pan with the sugar and six tablespoons of water and bring to the boil. Lower the heat and let the compote bubble gently for a few minutes until the berries have burst and the syrup is deep purple. Remove and set aside.

To serve, remove the weight, plate and clingfilm from the sieve. Turn the sieve upside down on a serving plate, shaking it gently to dislodge the cream from its container. Dust, if you wish, with a little icing sugar and orange zest. Serve with the cherry compote. *(continued)*

• I like to make the cherry compote just before serving, so the steaming fruit contrasts with the cool, milky ricotta cream.

• Blueberries, with their inky purple juice, will work well here, even more so with a spritz of lemon juice to lift their spirits.

STRAWBERRIES, PASSION FRUIT, BALSAMIC

Strawberries made to taste more intensely of themselves by the addition of a sweetly sharp dressing.

Serves 2

strawberries 250g

caster sugar 2 tablespoons

passion fruit 4

balsamic vinegar

Cut the strawberries in half and put them in a serving bowl. Scatter over the sugar. Slice the passion fruit in half, then empty them, with the aid of a teaspoon, into a tea strainer or small sieve. Spoon the passion fruit juice, discarding the seeds, over the berries, then add a couple of drops of balsamic vinegar. Fold everything gently together, taking care not to damage the berries, then set aside in a cool place for an hour before serving.

• The amount of balsamic vinegar is a matter of taste, but even the merest drop or two will add a deep, mellow note to the berries.
• Cutting the berries in half allows them to soak up more of the deeply fruity dressing.

PEACHES, BISCUITS, MASCARPONE

Ripe peaches. Soft, vanilla-scented, crumb-freckled cream cheese.

Serves 4

double cream 200ml
mascarpone 100g
vanilla extract a few drops
sweet, crumbly biscuits 75g

peaches, ripe 4
the zest of half an orange,
  finely grated
crystallised rose petals 8

Whip the cream until thick enough to hold its shape but no more than that. Add the mascarpone and a couple of drops of vanilla extract, but don't mix just yet.

Crush the biscuits to crumbs – a mixture of textures, from fine sand to coarse gravel. Add the crumbs to the cream and fold together gently, just enough to combine the cream and mascarpone with the crumbs.

Tear the peaches in half and discard the stones. Place a peach and a spoonful of the cream on each plate and add a scattering of orange zest and crystallised rose petals.

• Ripeness is all. This dish is for celebrating a fruit at its moment of perfection.
• The cream should be whipped only until it will sit in soft mounds. If it will stand in stiff peaks, it will be over-whipped and won't be able to take the addition of the mascarpone and crumbs without splitting.

WATERMELON, PROSECCO

The most refreshing of summer ices. For days when it is almost too hot to move.

Serves 8

elderflower cordial 125ml   prosecco 400ml
watermelon flesh 500g
   (skinned weight)

Pour the elderflower cordial into the jug of a blender or bowl of a food processor, add the watermelon, cut into chunks, and process to a purée. Scoop the scarlet slush into a freezer box and pour in the prosecco, stirring thoroughly. Cover and freeze for a good four hours.

To serve, run the tines of a fork across the surface of the frozen granita, ploughing up crystals of palest pink water ice and transferring them to cold glasses.

• You can use pink grapefruit juice instead of prosecco if you prefer. The hue will be gorgeous, like a late summer sunset.
• Chilled glasses – even lightly frozen if they are frost-proof – will make the granita sparkle all the more.

Index

Grand Marnier:
  sponge fingers, cherry, custard 290-2
granita:
  watermelon, prosecco 304
green beans:
  roasted pepper, tomato, focaccia 150
  tomatoes, beans, bread 186-8
green falafel, watermelon, yoghurt 136
greens, coconut curry 10
griddles 192
grills 192-3
guacamole:
  mustard guacamole, mozzarella,
    bagel 106

H
halloumi:
  halloumi, melon, chilli 202
  halloumi, mint, aubergine 78-80
  halloumi, tomatoes 128
harissa:
  tomatoes, couscous, harissa 160-2
hazelnuts:
  aubergine, hazelnuts, onions 122
  plums, brown sugar, hazelnuts 288
Henderson, Margot 166
herb butter 36-8
herb yoghurt 58
hobs 208
honey:
  aubergine, honey, sheep's cheese 56
  fig, goat's cheese, honey 276-8
  plums, croissants 260
horseradish:
  trofie, parsley, Pecorino 254
hummus 30

I
ice cream:
  lemon rice, mango, ice cream 272
  peach, blackberries, ice cream 284-6

K
kale, blue cheese, orecchiette 138

L
lasagne:
  broad beans, spring greens, lasagne 154-6
leeks:
  broad beans, flageolets, courgettes 216
lemon:
  fettucine, samphire, lemon 234
  lemon rice, mango, ice cream 272
lentils:
  burrata, broccoli, lentils 172
  lentils, peppers, Gorgonzola 140-2
lettuce:
  grilled lettuce, carrot soup 196

M
mangoes:
  lemon rice, mango, ice cream 272
marrow:
  marrow, tomato, couscous 82-4
  marrow, za'atar, herb yoghurt 58
marzipan:
  blackberry, apple, marzipan 262-4
mascarpone:
  peaches, biscuits, mascarpone 302
  ricotta, orange blossom, cherries 296-8
melon:
  halloumi, melon, chilli 202
  melon, peppers, cucumber 12
  watermelon, prosecco 304
meringue, apricots, blackcurrants 282
milk:
  lemon rice, mango, ice cream 272
mint:
  halloumi, mint, aubergine 78-80
  herb butter 36-8
miso:
  asparagus, miso, mustard 212
  miso, cauliflower, ginger 14

potatoes, spinach, pomegranate 182
potatoes, wild garlic 240
roast new potatoes, spinach sauce 148
spring cabbage, spring onions,
    potatoes 88–90
prosecco:
    watermelon, prosecco 304
puddings 258–9
puffed rice:
    pomegranate, cucumber, puffed rice 32
pumpkin seeds:
    cauliflower, pumpkin seeds,
        breadcrumbs 228–30

Q
quinoa, peas, sprouted seeds 34

R
radishes:
    broad beans, couscous, pine kernels 218–20
    bulgur, nectarines, parsley 18
    fennel, radish, yoghurt 174
    gnocchi, tomato, radishes 74–6
    papaya, carrots, radish 22–4
    tomatoes, peas, feta 184
ras el hanout:
    freekeh, avocado, chives 236–8
raspberries:
    blackcurrant, yoghurt 266
    currants, gin, bread 280
redcurrants:
    currants, gin, bread 280
rice:
    beetroot, curry leaves, crisp onions 168
    lemon rice, mango, ice cream 272
    rice, broad beans, asparagus 36–8
    rice, courgettes, pickled vegetables 44
    rice, pickles, nori 46
    risotto 2–3
    (see also puffed rice)

rice cakes:
    peach, blackberries, ice cream 284–6
ricotta 111
    baked ricotta, asparagus 132
    broad beans, pea shoots, salted ricotta 170
    courgettes, ricotta, pine kernels 198–200
    cucumber, basil, cream cheese 274
    ricotta, orange blossom, cherries 296–8
risotto 2–3
rocket:
    mushrooms, peas, toast 176
runner beans, cashews, tomatoes 40

S
salads:
    broad beans, couscous, pine kernels
        218–20
    broad beans, pea shoots, salted
        ricotta 170
    bulgur, nectarines, parsley 18
    fennel, radish, yoghurt 174
    freekeh, avocado, chives 236–8
    freekeh, peaches, feta 8
    noodles, sprouted beans, peanuts 178–80
    papaya, carrots, radish 22–4
    pasta, tomatoes 70–2
    pomegranate, cucumber, puffed rice 32
    potatoes, spinach, pomegranate 182
    quinoa, peas, sprouted seeds 34
    runner beans, cashews, tomatoes 40
    tomatoes, beans, bread 186–8
    tomatoes, couscous, harissa 160–2
    tomatoes, peas, feta 184
salsa 136, 202
samphire:
    fettucine, samphire, lemon 234
sandwiches 98–9
    carrots, tomatoes, buns 100–2
    feta, beetroot, buns 104
    mustard guacamole, mozzarella,
        bagel 106

Acknowledgements

Food on a plate, words on a page. It is what I do. It is also what I love. Cooking, making myself and others something to eat, then writing about it. There isn't a day that I don't think how grateful I am that I can continue to do this.

That said, a collection of recipes such as this is always a collaborative affair and I am immensely appreciative of that. A dish I might throw together for supper on a still summer's evening will only appear on the page after it has been tested, photographed and edited with the help of others. I would never want to work alone, in what could amount to a creative vacuum. To do so could risk culinary atrophy, your cooking losing its sense of fun and spirit, and therefore, I would argue, its point.

The best days of all are those when I cook with others. Particularly those when my business partner and producer James Thompson comes over and we cook together. Much of my daily eating, the recipes in this book, not to mention my television programmes, are the product of that long and happy collaboration. Thank you, James.

Before we sit down and eat (we eat every recipe, it is one of the perks of doing what I do), everything is photographed by Jonathan Lovekin, who has worked with me for thirty years. We don't cook or style the recipes specially for photography. We cook to eat. Neither do we use 'props', which is why many of the plates and bowls may seem familiar, turning up in several of my books, like old friends. They are part of my kitchen and therefore my everyday eating.

Many of those plates and bowls have been made by potters whose work I admire, and I would like to thank them for letting me use them. In particular Florian Gadsby, Anne Mette Hjorthøj, Tony Gant, Darren Ellis, Lisa Hammond, Rupert Spira and Teppei Ono.

Some of the recipes in this volume have appeared before in my weekly column in the *Observer Magazine* and I would like to thank Allan Jenkins, Harriet Green, Martin Love, Gareth Grundy, Molly Tait-Hyland and everyone at the *Observer* and *Guardian* for their kind and enduring support and patience over the last twenty-six years. I don't think I can ever thank them enough.

Others have played just as an important part in getting this collection of recipes to you. Louise Haines, Michelle Kane, Julian Humphries, Jack Smyth, Sarah Thickett and Chris Gurney at Fourth Estate, along with Annie Lee, Louise Tucker and Gary Simpson, many of whom have worked on my books for as long as I can remember. Thanks too, to my long-standing literary agent Araminta Whitley at LAW and to Rosemary Scoular at United Agents. Huge thanks are also due to Marina de Pass and Natalia Lucas. I love working with you all.

Shout-outs too to David Pearson for his wonderful design and gorgeous fonts and to Tom Kemp whose extraordinary work has made this and its accompanying autumn and winter volume so beautiful. To Dalton Wong and George Ashwell at Twenty Two Training and to Richard Stepney at Fourth Floor. I am grateful too to dear friends Tim d'Offay at Postcard Teas, Takahiro Yagi at Kaikado, Takako Saito, Tok and Hiromi Kise and to Maureen Doherty and everyone at Egg for their gentle inspiration and friendship.

My days would not be the same without the words, pictures and support from my followers on Instagram and Twitter and the enduring support of booksellers everywhere. I thank you one and all.

Nigel Slater, London, 2019

A note on the brushstrokes

It's rare that an author and a publisher are willing to take the plunge of working with an artist on the design of a book. So I was intrigued to get a call from book jacket designer, Jack Smyth, who wanted somehow to have a brushstroke running across the cover of the two *Greenfeast* books. At the first meeting, we all had a hugely lively conversation about what might be possible and, most importantly, what the brush could add to the ideas behind the books. Nigel was intrigued to find that my technique was an entirely Western one and is the root of all our classical Roman typefaces. The capital letter E in this sentence owes its entire underlying shape to the way the E was written with five brushstrokes on buildings in ancient Rome. He showed me several paintings on his walls and we realised that most of them featured really strong, individual brushstrokes.

The initial task was to find strokes that would work on the two front covers. My first thought for the *Spring, Summer* book was something with a sudden, joyful start, reflecting the startling speed of the new growth of plants, succulence, leafiness, reaching for the light. Then the second book could have something heavier, slower, coming to a stop: like a branch drooping with fruit and the end of growth during winter. Designs and printing suggestions flew back and forth and it worked out best to have a single stroke for both books, combining each idea. Around this time, the book designer, David Pearson, thought it would make sense to have brushwork running throughout the interior of the books. There followed a dance of text and stroke with each of us trying to help the other make it all work together.

There's an essence in a single brushstroke. In a way, it is the capturing of the very time spent making it, since all one's energy and focus and intent, for those few seconds, are directed into conjuring the stroke to appear. *Greenfeast* is about time: the great clock cycle of our solar orbit, changing the food which is available, and the miniature rhythm of our planet's spin, making us ask the simple question, 'What shall I eat today?'

The brushstrokes on and in this book don't represent anything. They are not pictures of things. They're just a small aside, a little interference to remind you about the nature of nature, where, ultimately, the food in this book comes from. Natural laws apply at all levels and the movement of my arm, as a series of interlinked hinges, will always produce a stroke which has an affinity with the chaotic movement of water in a stream or the frozen turbulence of a tree's branches, or, indeed, the swirl of a spoon through a bowl of soup.

Tom Kemp

A note on the type

The text is typeset in Portrait, designed by Berton Hasebe in 2013. Portrait is a modern-day interpretation of the early Renaissance typefaces, first made popular in Paris and cut by Maître Constantin. His influence can be seen in the work of the famed punch cutters of the next generation, Claude Garamond and Robert Granjon, whose work is so familiar to modern day readers.

The cover type is set in Brunel, an English modern designed by Paul Barnes and Christian Schwartz in 2008. Brunel in turn was based on the first moderns issued by the Caslon foundry in 1796. The name is derived from the Anglo-French engineers Sir Marc and Isambard Kingdom Brunel.

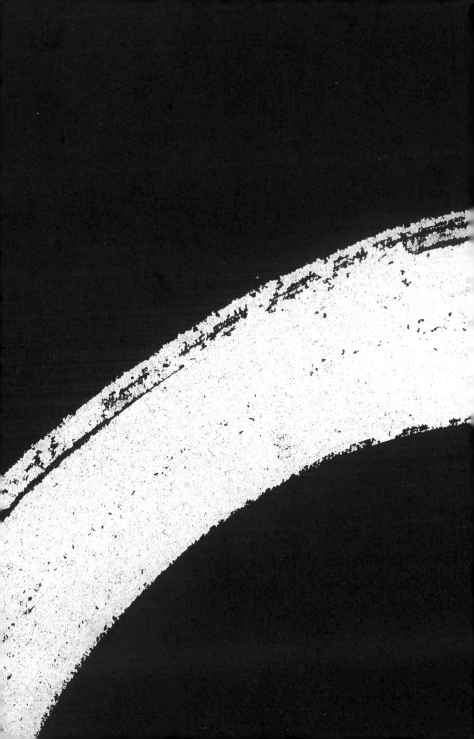